The Secret to Transformation

Within The Paradox

From Chaos to Clarity: The Science of Transformation & Inner Mastery

Edy M. Lopez

Contents

Dedication

For my mother,

Thank you for giving me life,

for the love you offered me,

and for the courage to speak.

For my father,

Thank you for showing me what

strength looks like

in our darkest moments,

and for sharing your wisdom with me.

Acknowledgements

There are many people I could thank, but one stands above all—my wife, Tatiana Sitnik. From the very first chapter I read to her, she believed in me. She encouraged me, stood by me, and gave me both the space and strength to keep going. Even after I lost my teaching job, she remained patient and unwavering as I worked ten hours a day for thirty days straight during that unusually cool July. Thank you, my love. This book would not exist without your belief in me.

To my daughters, Alexandra and Olivia—you are my inspiration, my purpose, and my reminder that transformation is always possible.

To my sisters, Lidia and Liliana—my two rock stars. No matter what was happening in my life, you answered the phone when I needed you the most. Your love has been my anchor.

To Captain McGuire—thank you for recognizing the leader in me when everything else seemed to be falling apart. I made a promise you may have forgotten, but I intend to keep it.

To Retired Command Sergeant Major Johnson—thank you for believing in me the very first moment I walked into your company. You looked me in the eye, noticed the patches on my starched uniform and highly polished boots, and asked where I was from. "California," I answered. You pressed further, "No, what city?" "Inglewood, First Sergeant," I replied, standing at parade rest. In that instant, you understood my story. You then asked why I was still a Specialist (E-4), and without hesitation, you asked if I was ready for PLDC. "Roger that, First Sergeant," I said. That single exchange changed the course of my life; someone believed that I was worthy to lead others.

And finally, to every Veteran who has fought, is fighting, or will fight their demons—this book is for you. It's the claymore covering your six, ready to shred anything from your past that tries to sneak up and take you down. You've walked through hell with your fists clenched, heart pounding, and mind screaming—and you're still here. This book won't coddle you. It's not therapy. It's truth. A reminder that you're not broken—you're forged. I hope within these pages you find the strength, the clarity, and the fire you've been searching for.

Roger, Out.

United States Army SSG. Lopez — July 2008

About the Author

Edy Mayen Lopez is a transformational author, speaker, and educator whose work bridges science, spirituality, and the human experience. A U.S. Army veteran who served eight years in the military—including three deployments, one to Afghanistan and two to Iraq—with the 82nd Airborne Division and the 1st Infantry Division, Edy embodies resilience, discipline, and heart-centered leadership.

After completing his service, Edy earned his Bachelor's degree in Business Management and spent over two decades leading teams and organizations across multiple industries. He later became an educator, teaching English Language Development (ELD) for three years, where he excelled as an educator and earned several awards for his performance.

He is the founder of EdyTalks LLC and host of The Yogi Podcast – School of Transformation, where he explores consciousness, healing, and the evolution of self.

From a six-month spiritual awakening marked by intense panic attacks and inner collapse, Edy intensified his studies in the mind, emotion, and energy. That journey became the foundation of Within the Paradox—a book that unites science, trauma recovery, and spiritual realization into one path of healing and awakening.

Today, he teaches that true freedom begins when we realize we are not our thoughts or emotions, but the awareness behind them. Through his writing, speaking, and coaching, Edy guides others toward peace, purpose, and higher consciousness.

Edy wrote this book as a mirror—for those ready to face themselves, to heal what hurts, and to remember the light that has always been within.

Introduction

> **"The more you know, the more you realize you don't know."**
>
> — *Aristotle*

What happens when you have no choice but to modify, change, or completely transform your life?

What happens when waking up becomes a chore?

When breathing feels like a burden and the beat of your heart becomes tired of drumming?

This isn't just a philosophical question. It was my reality. My life.

I spent years walking through life with a storm inside my head. A silent war between who I appeared to be and what I was actually carrying. Like millions of people around the world, I was searching for motivation or a three-step plan to success. But in reality, I was searching for relief from the pain and pressure from myself.

I did not author this book because I mastered anything. I wrote it because for years, since I was stationed in the 82nd Airborne Division, I spent almost every day at Barnes & Noble sipping Caramel Frappuccinos and consuming books after books, not knowing why. From Socrates to Thoreau, from Gandhi to Descartes, Nietzsche, Aristotle, Thomas Aquinas, Freud, Jung, and Sri Aurobindo—from the Egyptians to the Mayans, the Koran, the Bible, and the Bhagavad Gita—my life unfolded as a vast colosseum of masters, each voice echoing through the corridors of time, imparting fragments of an integral wisdom that shaped the architecture of my soul. And 10 years later, after leaving the 1st Infantry Division at Fort Riley, the notification calls of fellow veterans taking their lives began to ring my phone… And I learned the why of my book. But to write this book, I had to face what was breaking me and undergo what felt like my last breaths of life. I had to face the same demons my friends were fighting. I am certainly not a guru or some saint. I don't claim to know anything or to teach anyone anything, and I do not have fancy degrees in any of the Sciences. Simply put, this is my story, how I survived the War within.

I am the reciprocating effect of trauma at its best. And I am also the proof that those experiences we encounter in life do not have to be the end of our story.

This book is for the eight billion souls on this planet who are searching for something more—something real. For those seeking understanding. For those with or without success. Whether you're a business leader trying to better your game, a teacher trying to stay grounded, a veteran fighting PTSD, a parent trying to stay patient, in recovery trying to stay alive, a seeker trying to remember who you are, or on death row from your mind like I was—this book is for you.

Inside these pages, you will find pieces of my story, yes—but more importantly, you'll find mirrors. Reflections. And questions. Language for the parts of yourself you've struggled to name, and a raw testimony encapsulated in a reality pill. You'll learn about energy, trauma, emotion, the nervous system, consciousness, physics, and what it means to transform—not just emotionally or spiritually, but somatically, mentally, and physically. You will learn the pre-intricacies of leadership and not post-lesson leadership mentalities.

You'll be challenged to look at what you've carried. To question what you've accepted and learn to call "normal." To feel what you've buried. And to reclaim the parts of yourself that were never lost—only forgotten.

If you are holding on by a thread, I honor you. If you are grieving, healing, searching, waking up—you're not alone. If you've made it this far in life without feeling safe in your own body, this book is for you. If you're seeking to up your game and become a lighthouse of awareness, this book is also for you.

I can't promise that reading these pages will fix everything.

But I can promise that if you stay open, if you stay honest, and if you stay with yourself through the discomfort, you will begin to see the truth I discovered:

You are not broken.

You are becoming.

And that's more than enough to begin again.

With all my love and humanity—

OM. Amen. Amini.

Prologue

> **"I know that I know nothing."**
>
> — *Socrates*

A gun pressed against my head, hanging from a tree, or driving off a bridge and collapsing into the frigid water. Those were my three obsessive thoughts. To end it. These thoughts consumed the very life out of me every time they crossed my mind. For years, I saw glimpses of my death as if something kept calling me, saying in a silent vision, "die, die." The emotional roller-coaster frightened the shit out of me, and the more I saw those visions. The more fear entered my body. The more tense I became, the more my thoughts circled around this idea. I remember pacing through my house, consumed only with the thought, thinking of doing it, imagining it, and trying to process what it would look like. I was afraid of being home alone. I was afraid of going to sleep. Although at times, sleep was the only thing that kept me away from my thoughts. Every other day, it was a different scenario, and the more I resisted thinking about how I would do it, the more fear took over me. Being in this state is an area in life where you need to dig your heels deep into the ground if you want to survive. And if you're not mentally fit to understand the complexity of your mind. You will act on your thoughts. This part of my life, I call it awakening, and it was the most revealing six months that I will never forget. I will never forget, not because I was traumatized by these events. However, it was a traumatizing experience. I will never forget because it taught me more than 1,000 psychology books put together. Having experience with each thought. Each emotion. Each feeling. The visions that I now have are a completely different perspective on how the mind works. I now know from firsthand experience our capacity to overcome and override the mind. And eventually learning that my visions of death were perfectly normal, I was just ill-prepared to understand what was happening to me. So to make it utterly clear, this book is not about suicide;

it's about everyone's moment of truth in life, where you have to enter that fatal funnel and make the decision to sprout the best version of yourself or allow the circumstances of your mental chatter to dictate your life. It's about that moment in life when shit hits the fan and you're forced to step up to the plate to meet the future version of yourself and divorce the narrative of the old story holding you back.

At times, I did consider 5150 myself. Several times, I called the veterans' suicide hotline and was asked to schedule an appointment to see someone. Did I say anything about my thoughts? Of course. I was in pain. But I was a mastermind by explaining how aware I was and the work I had been putting in to better myself. Perfect self-manipulation. I remember after that initial phone call with the suicide hotline, I went straight to the backyard and started pulling weeds from the fence line to stop these thoughts in my head. I was trying anything to coexist with myself. I was alone. I felt alone. I was scared. I would have done anything to make all those thoughts go away. I became so tunnel-focused on only pulling each weed. Literally. Weed by weed. All because I did not want to hear my mind. I was in shorts, on my knees, trying to stay focused only on one thing: pulling weeds out. The pain in my knees did not phase me. Rocks, pine needles, nothing could make me feel pain. My only intent was to stop these feelings in my body. When I finally sat down with help a few days later, I was prepared to spill the beans and share my deepest thoughts. But life had other plans.

What I didn't realize was that the first visit wasn't meant for deep conversation. It was just to set up services. I still remember that day vividly. I had built up the courage to finally open up, only to find the social worker focused on paperwork and procedures rather than my story. I asked the social worker, "How can I 5150 myself?" and the only thing I heard was, "They will keep you for a week, and you will have to take the prescribed medications." It was at that moment that my mind screamed, "Fuck no!" Because already the medications they prescribed at the hospital were making me worse. I remember coming home after the ER feeling better, and as soon as I ingested the prescribed medications, I would start getting worse. Feeling down. Psychotic. Crazy. The sensations of death.

So here's how it at all started. On August 4th, 2022, I woke up like any other day – getting ready for work with the feeling of what the fuck am I doing with my life. Around this time, I had already left several jobs because I could not connect anymore. My professional life was falling apart. Fast. Although everywhere I worked, I had found much success and received immediate praise. My problems were never because of my performance. The problem was my heart; I gave my all in every job, but the jobs were not fulfilling enough to stay. I needed something bigger than myself. Somehow, I knew internally that I needed more complex challenges. Something that would challenge me and keep me busy for years. However, by this time, I knew well how my mind worked. And I, was on the hunt for it. Looking back, I see how subconsciously my heart knew, yet consciously I could not bring myself to understand what was happening.

On that morning, I woke up demoralized because I found myself working alone in a friend's office. The pay was fine, but I was trapped. I felt empty. I was constantly questioning myself to figure out where things went wrong. What's going on with me? Why is this happening to me? That day, as I made it to my job, I called my sister and spoke for 20 minutes or so. I explained to her that I was done with my spiritual life. I was done trying to understand this concept of consciousness, as it was draining my life; it wasn't taking me anywhere but keeping me still. My words specifically were, "I'm done with this spiritual bullshit, I'm taking charge of my life." We finished the conversation. I finished the last few tasks pending at work, and I drove away. Perhaps somewhat frustrated. As I drove, I changed my mind midway about lunch and instead began driving home. Suddenly, the symptoms of my new life began to kick in. Maybe it was the end. The beginning? I certainly had no idea what was about to hit me, like a train going 100 miles per hour. With 100s of wagons filled with cargo. Tankers filled with petroleum and liquid nitrogen, to catch me on fire immediately and extinguish me frozen. The perfect ambush. The paradox within.

As I drove down Harbor Boulevard, suddenly I started yawning heavily and felt super fatigue. A minute later. I started sighing as if I was running out of oxygen, but I felt composed. I'm ok. I'll recover. Focus. Drive.

Instinctually, I felt there was something wrong, and a voice in me said, "Rush to the hospital, this is going to get bad." As I merged into the freeway, I kept my calm, I stayed cool and collected. The goal was to make it to the VA Mather Medical Hospital and get myself checked in. I began to lower the window. A few minutes into the freeway, I felt like I needed air. The yawning got worse and worse to the point where I could not yawn enough to catch my breath. Three to five minutes later, I dialed... "911". Operator asked, "What's your emergency?" I said, "I can't breathe, I'm on the freeway, I'm slowing down, I'm pulling over near the Broadway exit, stay on the phone with me." Hysterically I began to almost scream "I can't breathe, I can't breathe, I think I'm having a heart attack, I'm going to pass out." As I stayed on the phone with the operator we agreed that I would reroute to the Davis Memorial Hospital. During that phone call, I thought, *this is it for me. I may possibly die.* I began swerving from lane to lane. I cracked the door open, ready to come out and lie on the ground. To be found fast in case I am still alive and be taken to the hospital. Eventually, I made it to the hospital parking lot. Parked my truck in the emergency lane. Walked inside and jumped in front of the line. Every breath felt like an hour, and as I stood looking at people in line, I realized how full of shit we all are when we go to the emergency room, not unless it's a real emergency. For that moment, I thought, *Wow, I am going through a real emergency.* Eventually, a nurse came around the desk, sat me down, and asked me to wait. I was like... wait? What. I can't breathe. And I started to feel like passing out. Within minutes, I was taken inside for an EKG and other medical exams. The nurses concluded I was fine. Sat me in a wheelchair. Classified my emergency as a non-emergency and threw me in the lobby to wait. I finally grew tired of waiting for hours, so I called my wife to escort me to the VA Mather Medical Hospital, where, as soon as I arrived, I was on a bed with wires all over my body. Finally, someone took me serious. Exam after exam. I finally felt safe.

After four hours, they could not tell me what was wrong, as some of the symptoms were chest pain, numbness in both arms, legs, hands, rapid heartbeat. Part of my face was tingling, I would start to lose my breath again, and I would feel dizzy as hell. They xrayed my lungs and scanned the rest of my body as well. For six hours, doctors were baffled trying to figure out what the hell was going on. Everything seemed to check out ok. Blood. EKG. Oxygen. Until the cardiologist checked me out and said my heart was clear. The ER doctors began to say that it could be anxiety or a panic attack. I asked, "What the hell is a panic attack? How did I get a panic attack? I was driving. Minding my own business. I wasn't doing anything strenuous. My life seems normal. In control. My mind could not reconcile this preposterous idea. A panic attack? Me? Not me? This can't be a panic attack. This is not a panic attack." My mind was in survival mode, trying to make sense of this event.

Six hours later, my symptoms subsided for a moment. Just enough for doctors to feel comfortable enough to release me. My mind was still trying to consolidate and reorganize. Trying to understand. Come up with a logical explanation. I left the ER completely lost, confused, wondering what had just happened to me. However, the panic attack symptoms had calmed down just enough to regain my sanity. I was going home, and I was released with a follow-up to see the cardiologist and a sleep study. An appointment to check my liver and my kidneys, and an array of other exams. Essentially, still no answers. Uncertainty.

After leaving the ER, I asked my wife to stop by a nearby restaurant. For the past three weeks, I had been fasting, and after the panic attack, I was left spent. I was not so hungry. But worried that perhaps what my body needed was food. My mind was still racing, trying to figure out if my emergency had something to do with the excess workouts and fasting. About three to four weeks prior to the panic attack, I made the decision to gain back control of my life. I began to work out. Too fast. Meditate. Refocus again. I had reached a point in life where I needed to change. I needed to start. Something needed to give because slowly I had been committing professional and personal suicide. So I thought, I need to get back to running. Run 4-8 miles per day like the old days. But in hindsight, I see that something worked. Whatever I was searching for. Arrived. I lifted the lid of Pandora's box on that August day, and carved into its edge were words that chilled me to the bone: Get ready, Edy. I will dismantle you piece by piece, expose every darkest shadow you've buried, and from your ruins, sculpt the best version you've ever known. This was the beginning to the end I was longing for. Finally, it had arrived.

The lie I was living unconsciously—the same lie we all feed ourselves and present to the world as reality—was coming to an end.

What you are about to read is not a memoir, though I share pieces of my story. It is a culmination of research I conducted before and during some of the most difficult moments of my life, often feeling like a lab rat in my own experiment. I would never recommend this path to anyone, yet at the time, I believed I had no other choice.

Within the Paradox is a manual for transformation. It is the meeting point of science, spirituality, and lived experience. It reveals the anatomy of awakening: how trauma is stored in the body, how thoughts shape energy, how emotion creates vibration, and how frequency governs the reality we experience. It is both explanation and invitation—a guide for those who are ready to step beyond survival and into awareness.

Across these pages, you will walk with me through the landscapes of mind and memory, the chambers of emotion, the wiring of the nervous system, and the language of energy that science is only beginning to name. You will see how consciousness evolves through stages—how the collapse of identity becomes the seed of rebirth, and how pain, when understood, becomes a teacher rather than a punishment.

This book does not promise a quick fix. It offers something deeper: understanding. It is designed to help you see your own process with new eyes—to recognize the mechanics of suffering and the pathways of healing within yourself. You will learn how to transmute energy, transcend thought, and transform the patterns that have kept you bound to old realities.

I have written this work as both a map and a mirror.

The map reveals the terrain of transformation—the structure, the science, the process.

The mirror reflects your own awakening as you move through it.

If you read with openness, you will not only understand these words—you will feel them. You will sense the same intelligence that guided me through darkness beginning to stir within you. That movement is not a coincidence; it is consciousness remembering itself.

So take a deep breath.

BEFORE

From 2017 to 2022

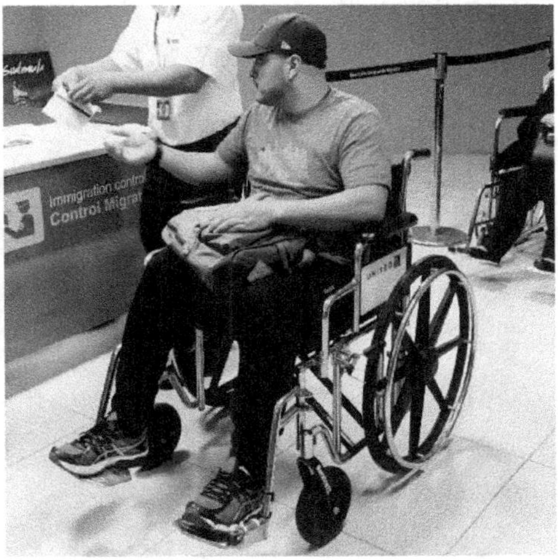

Recovering from a bulging disk in 2017.

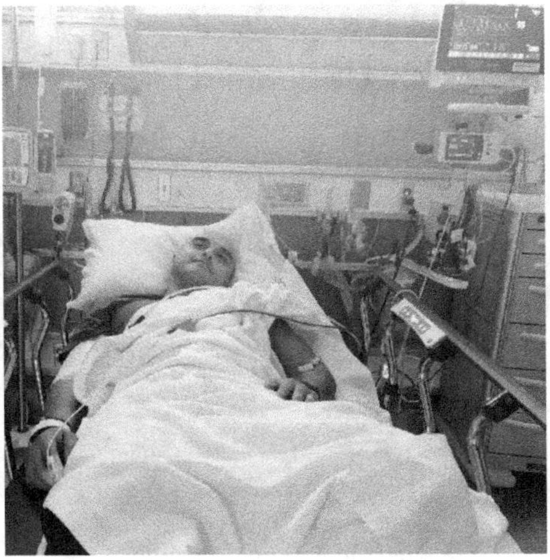

Bulging disk ER visit, 2017.

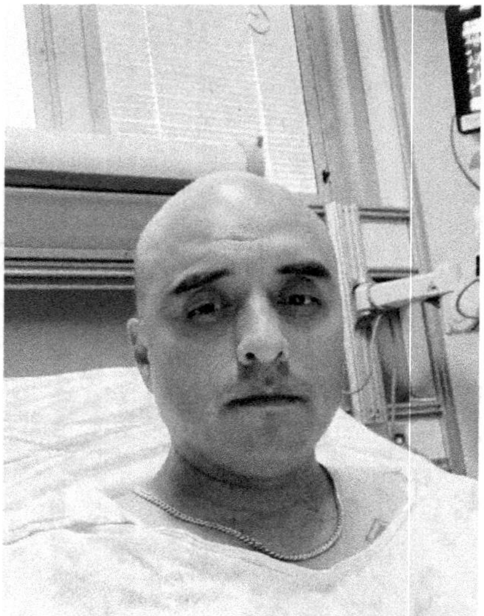

First panic attack on August, 2022

Weighing around 200 LBS in 2022.

Chapter One
Darkness

> **"The darker the night, the brighter the stars."**
>
> — *Fyodor Dostoevsky*

Confronting my darkness was not a choice made lightly, nor was it a decision born from a single moment of clarity—it was the inevitable crossing of a threshold where the weight of existence pressed so hard upon my chest that breathing became both an act of defiance and an act of surrender, where every thought felt like a blade and every second like a battlefield. It was, for lack of a gentler word, the breaking of all illusions, the collapse of every structure I thought was holding me together, the ultimate ambush of the mind. And in that collapse, when everything I clung to disintegrated into fragments too sharp to hold, I realized there was no escape route, no detour, no magic pill to dull the truth: the only way out was through.

This was the crucible of my life, the moment that burned everything false so something real could emerge, though at the time, I could not articulate it that way. Back then, all I knew was the chaos, the rage, the unbearable heaviness inside a mind that no longer felt like mine. Doctors, psychologists, and social workers all offered the same lifeline disguised as logic: "Take the pills. They will make you feel better." And maybe for someone else, those words would have sounded like hope. For me, they felt like a coffin with soft pillows, a slow burial beneath the weight of sedation. So I refused. I clenched my jaw against the easy escape and said, without hesitation, "No!"

What followed were six months that felt like six lifetimes, months where nights bled into days and days into nights without distinction, where the ugliest corners of my mind revealed themselves without mercy, where I faced thoughts that made me recoil, that made me wonder how a human being could carry such darkness and still draw breath. It was not poetic. It was not romantic. It was raw and vulgar and filled with images I will never fully describe, because to do so would be to drag you into a room most people never dare enter—a room that exists inside all of us, whether we admit it or not. This was the dark night of the soul, that infamous passage mystics speak of, except nothing about it felt mystical when you're the one choking on the silence of your own despair.

And yet, even as I write this, I know there will be two of you reading these words. The first is the egoic reader: the one who parses these sentences, who seeks meaning, who categorizes and judges, who wants to turn this chaos into a neat philosophy because that feels safer than truth. The second is the quiet reader: the one hiding beneath your ribs, the one who flinches when old memories surface, the one who has been silenced for so long by layers of noise and interpretation that it no longer believes it has a voice. The ego will do its job. It will scan these words for safety, for familiarity, for the assurance that nothing here will threaten its control. But this book is not written for the ego. It is written for the other one, the buried one—the living, breathing organism within you that is desperate to be free.

If you feel resistance rising as you move through these lines, let it rise. Let the judgments come. Let the discomfort wash over you like a tide you cannot stop. This is the cost of confronting the ugly, the unspoken, the raw truth most of us keep buried under layers of performance and pretense. And yet—and this is the paradox—it is not ugly at all. It is not darkness as the world defines it. It is the opposite of death; it is life in its most primal form. Because when you walk through this threshold, when you dismantle every story you've told yourself about who you are and what you deserve, the only thing left standing is the essence that has no name. The nothingness. The still point. And from that nothingness emerges the most exquisite thing you will ever encounter: your own consciousness, unmasked, unchained, untamed.

What you are stepping into now is not just a chapter—it is a paradox so vast that philosophers have drowned in its waters for centuries. It is the enigma that dissolves certainty and demands surrender. And at the heart of this paradox lies a truth you may not yet be ready to accept: within every fragment of decay, within every crack in the structure you thought would hold forever, there is a pulse. A life force. Call it flow. Call it the zone. Call it God. Call it whatever helps you sleep at night. But know this: it is real. And it is moving through you now, even as you sit here, eyes scanning this page, heart thudding with questions you cannot yet name.

The Mind

The mind is the most seductive thing you will ever encounter, and it will either be your greatest ally or the most elaborate illusion you will ever fall for. People speak of it casually, as if the mind were simply a tool they pick up when needed, as if it were a loyal servant waiting patiently to fulfill their will, yet nothing could be further from the truth. The mind is not passive—it is alive, pulsating, scheming, constructing narratives at every moment, whispering and sometimes screaming, shaping the contours of reality so convincingly that you would swear the picture it paints is the absolute truth. And if you have lived long enough, you already know the cruel paradox: the mind can build kingdoms, but it can also burn them to ash before you've had a chance to breathe their air.

When I speak of the mind, I don't mean only thought, though thought is often the mask it wears most clearly. I am speaking of a force—a ceaseless stream of interpretation, categorization, judgment, prediction—a river that never stops moving. If you have ever tried to still it, you know the futility of that attempt. Close your eyes for five seconds, and watch. You will see thought after thought cascading like dominoes, each one triggering the next, each one clamoring for attention as if the survival of the entire universe depended on its urgency. This is the ride most people never question; the ride they assume is life itself.

And so we try to improve it. We fill bookshelves with manuals on positive thinking, affirmations, manifestation, and neural rewiring, as if the mind could be trained like a dog that only needs treats and repetition. But here is the unspoken truth: the mind is not yours to train in that way. You can discipline it, yes. You can guide it, yes. But to think you own it—that it belongs to you—is the first and most seductive illusion. The mind is ancient. It carries echoes of every ancestor who fought to survive, every fear encoded in the marrow of human evolution. And when you try to bend it to your will without understanding it, you are like a child demanding obedience from a hurricane.

This is why I insist on this: before you can hope to master anything—your habits, your emotions, your so-called destiny—you must first understand this organism inside your skull. Because right now, if you are honest, you do not control your mind; it controls you. It dictates how you wake up, what you feel when you look in the mirror, what you believe is possible for you, how you love, how you fight, how you fail. It is the architect of your joy and the saboteur of your peace, often in the same breath.

But understanding the mind is not a weekend project. It is not a tidy checklist of hacks you can complete between sips of morning coffee. It is a lifelong unfolding, a dismantling of illusions so layered that most never make it past the first peel. And yet, this dismantling is the very thing you were born for. Because to live as a human being is not merely to exist—it is to become conscious of existence itself.

Being human is not about survival. Your mind may try to convince you otherwise. Being human is about expansion, about tasting the marrow of life with awareness so sharp it cuts through the numbness of habits, about asking not just how to live but what living even means. And for that, you must become intimate with the currents of your own mind, not in theory but in practice—in the silence of your own breath, in the storm of your own chaos, in the raw confrontation with thoughts so dark you flinch when they surface.

This is why I say: the mind is the sexiest thing on Earth if you learn how it works. Because once you do, once you pierce through its illusions and see the gears turning, you realize you are not the machinery—you are the one who observes it. And that realization is liberation. But until then, brace yourself, because this ride—the one you've been on since birth without even knowing it—is about to take you into the deepest corners of yourself.

As we enter this chapter, I am asking for something radical. I am asking you to keep your mind open—not just cracked at the edges, but flung wide like a door unhinged by wind. What does that mean? It means you will have to let go of certainty, of the comfort of neat definitions, of the impulse to box everything into right and wrong, true and false, good and bad. It means you will have to walk straight into paradox, into questions that feel like riddles, into truths that sound like contradictions, and resist the urge to turn back.

Because what I am about to show you is not a tidy set of rules. It is a Pandora's Box wrapped in curiosity, and if you dare to lift the lid, your life will never look the same. So buckle in. Loosen your grip on what you think you know. And when the ground beneath you start to quake—and it will—let it. Because only by falling can you learn to rise in a way that is real.

Non-Duality

What happens if I told you that everything you've been taught about good and bad, light and dark, success and failure, was nothing more than a convenient myth—a story repeated so many times it became a truth we never stopped to question? What if I told you that the universe does not speak in absolutes, that it knows nothing of your rigid categories, that life itself is not divided into black and white but painted in gradients so subtle the human mind, in its hunger for control, collapses them into opposites for the sake of comfort? Would that unsettle you? Would it shake the scaffolding you've built to hold yourself upright in a world that terrifies you with its uncertainty?

Because here is the truth: reality is non-dual. There are no perfect opposites battling for supremacy across some cosmic chessboard. There are degrees, and those degrees are illusions of separation that dissolve the moment you look closely enough. Heat and cold are not enemies—they are temperatures on the same spectrum. Love and hate are not strangers—they are currents of the same river, their intensity differing only by direction. Life and death are not contradictions—they are phases of a single process too vast for the mind to map without distorting it into a story.

The mind resists this. It thrives on categories because categories mean control, and control is the drug the ego cannot live without. To tell the ego that good and bad are the same essence in disguise is to strip it of its favorite game. Because when the illusion of duality collapses, what becomes of judgment? What becomes of superiority? What becomes of the narrative that says, "I am good because I am not like them"? It shatters. And when it shatters, so does the identity built upon it. This is why people cling so desperately to absolutes—they are life rafts in an ocean of ambiguity.

But if you can let go—just for a moment—something extraordinary happens. The veil lifts, and you see the mechanics of reality for what they are: movement, flow, transition. You see that what you once called failure was only a bend in the road, a necessary detour in the architecture of growth. You see that what you labeled as darkness was not an enemy but a teacher—harsh and uncompromising, yes, but precise in its intention to strip you of illusions that no longer serve you.

When you stop dividing life into warring halves, you begin to taste its wholeness, and in that wholeness lies freedom. Because if good and bad are the same essence, then every so-called mistake was never a mistake—it was a step. Every heartbreak was not punishment—it was initiation. Every loss was not annihilation—it was clearing space for what needed to decompose so the new self could bloom. And yet we fight this with a ferocity that exhausts us, as if clinging to the corpse of who we were could keep us from becoming who we are meant to be.

This is why duality was never the enemy—it was the illusion. The illusion that tells you joy cannot exist without pain, that abundance is impossible without lack, that to experience love you must first taste heartbreak. These are half-truths born from a mind that cannot comprehend the infinite, so it reduces infinity into digestible binaries. But life is not binary. It is a spectrum, a continuum, a field where everything belongs. And when you understand this—not intellectually, but viscerally—you stop resisting the very experiences designed to shape you.

Imagine, for a moment, what your life would feel like if you stopped labeling every event as good or bad. If you stopped assigning meaning based on fear. If you allowed things to be as they are without the weight of judgment crushing them into something smaller than they were meant to be. Would that not feel like liberation? Would it not feel like peace? Because peace is not the absence of chaos—it is the absence of resistance. And resistance is born from the illusion of duality.

The moment you accept that there is no battle to win—that every experience is simply life seeking to know itself through you—you drop the sword. You stop fighting. You start flowing. And in that flow, you find the singularity—the point where opposites collapse, where life ceases to be a problem to solve and becomes an experience to witness.

So as we move forward, remember this: duality is a lens, not a law. It is a story your mind tells to make sense of what terrifies it. But stories can be rewritten. And the story of your life—the story of who you are and what this all means—begins to change the moment you realize there was never an enemy to fight, only a mirror reflecting you back to yourself.

Information, Knowledge, Learning, & Understanding

To live is to experience, and experience is nothing more than the condensation of infinite possibilities into a single moment that demands your attention. But how do we interpret these moments? How do we take the raw texture of life—the sights, the sounds, the sensations—and turn them into something we can name, something we can hold without drowning in its magnitude? The answer lies in the architecture of the mind, in the four processes that silently shape every layer of your reality: information, knowledge, learning, and understanding.

Most people use these words interchangeably, tossing them around in conversations like loose coins, unaware of the weight they carry, unaware of the distinctions that could liberate them if only they took the time to see. But here is the truth: these processes are not the same, and if you misunderstand them, you misunderstand yourself. So let us slow down. Let us dissect what happens every time life enters through your senses, every time reality brushes against your skin and demands interpretation.

Learning is the entry point—the open gate through which experience flows into you. From the moment you were born, your senses became portals, digesting the world in fragments of light, vibration, sound, taste, and touch. A newborn does not know what a mother is; it only knows warmth, scent, and heartbeat. Those impressions become patterns, and those patterns form the foundation of learning. Learning, then, is not an achievement; it is a reflex. It is how life moves into you, how the outside world begins to inscribe itself upon the slate of your nervous system.

When those inscriptions accumulate, they become a knowing, knowledge. Knowledge is what you "know," or at least what you think you know, because knowledge is simply organized memory. It is the catalog your mind creates to give shape to chaos, the filing system that turns experience into information, data into concepts, concepts into beliefs. And while knowledge feels like power—and in many ways it is—it is also a trap, because knowledge, by its nature, is static. It freezes a living process into a dead form, and then convinces you that the form is reality.

This is why people cling to knowledge like it is the ultimate truth, when in fact it is the echo of something that once lived. Knowledge is yesterday's weather report in a world where the sky changes every second. And yet, without knowledge, we would drown in immediacy. So knowledge serves a purpose—but only if you understand its limitations.

Understanding, however, is an entirely different dimension. Understanding does not live in the past. Understanding is alive, fluid, and immediate. It does not clutch at memory like a miser hoarding coins; it moves like water through the terrain of the present moment, observing, interpreting, and letting go. Where knowledge seeks to hold, understanding seeks to flow. Knowledge is accumulation; understanding is release. And release is what sets you free.

But here is the paradox—the one that keeps you bound in circles of confusion: your ego does not want understanding. It wants certainty. Certainty feels safe because uncertainty feels like death to the survival mind. So the ego clings to knowledge as if knowledge were life itself, when in truth, that clinging is the very thing that suffocates you. You think you need more information, more books, more seminars, more strategies, as if stacking fact upon fact will build you a bridge to peace. But the bridge you seek is not made of bricks—it is made of space. Space for awareness. Space for stillness. Space for what cannot be taught because it must be experienced.

This is why so many live their entire lives as libraries of facts yet remain strangers to themselves. They know the names of stars but have never sat still enough to feel the fire of their own existence. They can recite sacred texts yet have never tasted the silence from which those words were born. They chase knowledge the way addicts chase their next fix, mistaking accumulation for awakening, when awakening requires the opposite: an unclenching, a letting go so radical that the mind trembles at the thought of it.

True understanding arises not from mastering life, but from letting life reveal its truths in its own time. It is the surrender of control without the loss of awareness. It is not passivity—it is precision. Because when you understand, you are not sleepwalking through someone else's definitions; you are awake in the raw immediacy of now.

And this—this distinction between knowledge and understanding—is not a minor detail. It is the axis upon which transformation turns. Because if you mistake knowledge for understanding, you will drown in theory while starving for truth. You will confuse the map for the terrain, the menu for the meal, and the shadow for the light. And the tragedy is this: you will think you are living when you are only rehearsing life through secondhand concepts.

So pause here. Let this sink into the marrow of your being: you do not need more accumulation. You need awakening. And awakening does not happen in the past, because the past is memory, and memory is dead. Awakening happens in the living present, in the space between thoughts, in the silence your ego rushes to fill because silence terrifies it. Why? Because silence is the absence of story. And without a story, who are you?

The ego cannot answer that question without dying a little. But you can. And when you do, you will understand—not because I told you, not because you read it here, but because you tasted it yourself, in that space where knowledge collapses and understanding begins.

Good & Bad

If you strip life down to its bones—beyond the noise of culture, beyond the glitter of ambition, beyond the thousand masks you've been taught to wear—what you find at the core is not a war between good and evil, not some eternal tug-of-war between forces battling for your soul. What you find is something far simpler, yet infinitely more complex: an organism wired for survival, a nervous system designed to keep you alive at all costs, a mind that learned, long before you could speak, to label every experience as either safe or dangerous. And from that primitive equation—safety equals good, danger equals bad—the entire theater of human morality, judgment, and belief has unfolded.

Think about that for a moment. Everything you have ever called "good" or "bad" is nothing more than a meaning your mind assigned based on a sensation in your body. When something feels like expansion—when your chest opens, when your breath flows, when your muscles loosen—you call it good. When something feels like contraction—when your stomach knots, when your throat tightens, when your breath catches—you call it bad. And yet, both sensations arise from the same system: the intricate web of nerves pulsing through your body like a subterranean river, governed by nothing more mysterious than the ancient logic of survival.

Science calls it the autonomic nervous system, divided into sympathetic and parasympathetic branches, orchestrating the dance between fight and flight, and freeze. When you touch something hot, your hand jerks back before thought even enters the equation. That is survival in its purest form: immediate, instinctual, without analysis. But here is where the complexity begins: the same system that saved you on the day you almost fell as a child now fires alarms when you speak in public, when you risk rejection, when you dare to step into the unknown. The body does not distinguish between a physical threat and a psychological one. To the nervous system, danger is danger. And so fear becomes the compass that quietly rules your life, convincing you that discomfort is death, that change is fatal, that the unknown is an enemy waiting in the dark.

This is why so many people spend their lives chasing what feels safe, building empires of comfort, mistaking stagnation for stability. They call it "playing it smart," but what it really is is obedience to an ancient script written for a world of predators and prey. That script says: stay small, stay predictable, stay within the lines, because the unknown will kill you. And every time you obey, your world shrinks. Your possibilities narrow. And one day you wake up in a life that feels suffocating, wondering why happiness keeps slipping through your fingers even though you did everything "right."

I know this script intimately. I lived it. For years, I clung to the illusion that if I could just avoid the bad—if I could outrun the failures, sidestep the losses, stay one step ahead of the unknown—I would be safe. But safety is a cage with velvet bars. You do not notice you are imprisoned until the hunger for something more begins to gnaw at your bones, and by then, the cage feels permanent. That was me—clutching the bars, telling myself the world outside was too dangerous, that the cost of freedom was too high. But here is the paradox life shoved in my face: the bars were not real. The cage was an idea. And the key was in my hand the whole time.

The day I understood this—not intellectually, not as a concept, but as a visceral truth that shook me to my core—was the day the architecture of "good" and "bad" began to collapse. I realized that every event I had cursed as bad was, in hindsight, the very thing that carved me into who I am. The heartbreak I thought would kill me? It stripped me of illusions that were rotting me from the inside. The failures I swore were proof of my inadequacy? They were chisels, breaking away what was false so something stronger could emerge. Even the darkness—the panic, the nights I thought would never end—was not punishment. It was an initiation.

And if that is true for me, it is true for you. The labels you cling to—good, bad, right, wrong—are not absolutes. They are placeholders your mind uses to make sense of chaos; stories you tell yourself so you can breathe in a universe too vast for your comprehension. But stories can be rewritten. And when you rewrite the story of good and bad, you reclaim a power you did not know you lost: the power to meet life without resistance.

Imagine what that would feel like—not needing to push away the bad or cling desperately to the good. Imagine greeting every experience, not with judgment, but with curiosity: "What is this here to teach me? What is life asking of me now?" Do you feel the shift? Do you feel the weight sliding off your shoulders at the thought of no longer needing to control the uncontrollable? That is the beginning of freedom. Because freedom is not about arranging life into neat piles of good and bad. Freedom is about transcending the piles altogether, about seeing that life is not divided—it is whole. And wholeness is where peace lives.

So the next time your mind screams, "This is bad, this is wrong, this should not be happening," pause. Breathe. Ask yourself: "What if this, too, is part of the design?" Because it is. You may not see the pattern now. You may curse it, fight it, or try to escape it. But one day, you will look back and realize the thing you resisted was the very thing that opened the door. The door to growth. The door to strength. The door to a version of you that could not exist without this moment.

Good and bad are not truths. They are lenses. And when you remove the lenses, what remains is reality—not as you wish it to be, not as you fear it to be, but as it is. And that, my friend, is where life begins.

Overriding the Programming: Consciousness, Discipline, & Routines

There is a truth I need you to hold before we go any further, and it is this: the life you are living today is not a random arrangement of circumstances—it is a reflection of patterns, habits, and programs running so quietly beneath the surface that you rarely notice them. They are the loops that hum in the background, shaping what you think is possible, steering the choices you make before you even recognize them as choices. And unless you interrupt them, they will continue to define you.

But here is the gift in all of this: what was learned can be unlearned. What was wired in can be rewired. Your mind is not a fixed structure—it is an ever-changing landscape, alive with neuroplasticity, capable of forming new pathways every single day. That means every small, conscious choice is not trivial. It is an act of creation. It is a brushstroke on the canvas of the self you are becoming.

The first step is awareness—not as a fleeting thought, but as a practice of noticing. Begin to observe yourself in motion. Notice how your body reacts before your mind does. Notice the thoughts that rise when you are tired, when you are challenged, when you are afraid. Do this gently, without judgment, because judgment only reinforces the very patterns you are trying to release. Awareness is not about condemnation—it is about illumination. It is turning on the light in a room you've walked through in the dark for years, seeing clearly what was always there.

Once you see, the question becomes: how do you shift? This is where most people stumble, because they believe change must be dramatic to be real. But transformation rarely begins with explosions; it begins with small interruptions—tiny, deliberate acts that disrupt the flow of old patterns and invite something new to take root. A pause before the automatic yes. A breath before the habitual reaction. A choice to rise ten minutes earlier, not to conquer the world, but to sit with yourself in silence before the noise begins. These are not grand gestures. They are quiet revolutions.

This is why I speak of routines—not as rigid schedules meant to suffocate your freedom, but as structures that support your becoming. Habits happen unconsciously. They run in the background like old code. Routines, on the other hand, are conscious. They are intentional. They are the scaffolding that holds you steady as the old self begins to fall away. A routine is not about control—it is about alignment. It is how you weave presence into the fabric of your day so that you are not merely reacting to life but participating in its unfolding.

And yes, discipline will be required—not the harsh, punishing discipline you may have feared, but a softer, steadier kind. Discipline as devotion. Devotion to the life you know exists beyond the familiar. Devotion to the version of you that whispers from the edges of your awareness: I am here. Come find me. Discipline is not about force. It is about returning—again and again—to the choice you made when everything in you wanted to forget.

This will not always feel easy. There will be mornings when you want to go back to sleep, moments when the pull of the old feels stronger than the promise of the new. That is not failure. That is the nature of transition. Change unsettles the nervous system because it was designed for safety, and safety is in the known. So when fear rises—and it will—remember this: fear is not a stop sign. Fear is a signal that you are standing at the threshold of expansion. Let it guide you, not govern you.

And through it all, be patient. This is not a race. Transformation is not linear. Some days you will feel as though you are moving backward. You are not. You are spiraling upward in a way the mind cannot yet measure. Trust the process. Trust yourself. And above all, trust the truth that you are not here to live as a bundle of unconscious programs. You are here to live awake. To design a life that feels like yours—not because the world handed it to you, but because you chose it, breath by breath, step by step, moment by moment.

Fear & Transformation: Beyond Habits

Fear is a quiet visitor. It rarely knocks loudly at first; it slips in through the smallest cracks, a whisper behind your thoughts, a weight in your chest that feels like hesitation but is, in truth, something much older and deeper. Most of the time, fear does not arrive as terror—it arrives as reason, as logic, as the voice that says, not yet. Tomorrow will be better. You need more time. You need more certainty. And if you listen, you will wait forever because fear has one task and one task only: to keep you in the known.

The known feels safe because the unknown feels like death to the mind. And in a way, it is. Not the death of your body, but the death of your identity—the self you have carried, defended, and performed for so long. That is why transformation feels like grief sometimes. It feels like a loss, even when what you are losing is the very thing that has kept you from becoming. But let me offer you this: what feels like an ending is not destruction—it is clearing. It is the soft collapse of walls that no longer serve you, making space for a horizon you cannot yet see.

Fear is not your enemy. Fear is a compass. It points not toward danger but toward expansion. If you trace your fear to its edge, you will find the door to the life you have been asking for. And yes, you will tremble as you turn the handle. You will feel the urge to retreat. That is natural, because fear is the nervous system's way of saying, this is unfamiliar. We have never been here before. But unfamiliar does not mean unsafe. It means alive. It means you are standing on sacred ground—the threshold between the self you have known and the self you are becoming.

This is why the language of habits cannot hold the weight of transformation. Habits belong to the subconscious; they are loops that run without asking permission. And if you live by habits alone, you may polish the surface of your life while leaving its foundation untouched. Transformation is something else entirely. It is not the rearranging of behavior—it is the reimagining of being. It is not about adding layers; it is about peeling them back until what remains is raw and real and free.

And here is the part few speak of: this work will not be glamorous most days. It will feel quiet, ordinary, like a breath taken instead of a reaction given. It will feel like saying no to an old pattern when everything in you wants to say yes. It will feel like starting over a hundred times, because transformation is not a straight path—it is a spiral. You will revisit the same fears, the same doubts, not because you have failed, but because life is giving you a deeper mastery each time.

So when fear comes—and it will—do not run. Do not numb it. Do not pretend it is not there. Sit with it. Listen to it without obedience. Let it tell you what it came to tell you, then thank it for its service and take the step anyway. One small step. One breath forward. Because movement, not perfection, is what rewires a life.

And this is the moment where the crescendo begins, not as a roar but as a rising hum in your bones: You were not born to rehearse the same day until time runs out. You were not born to be ruled by a mind that clings to safety as if safety were life itself. You were born to expand, to stretch beyond what you thought was possible, to become the fullest expression of the life that pulses inside you. Fear will walk with you as you do this, but let it walk behind you—not ahead of you. Let it remind you that the edge you stand on is not an ending but a beginning.

And when that quiet question comes, as it always does—Will you step through?—Let your answer be yes. Not because the fear has vanished, but because something deeper has awakened in you: the knowing that the life you seek will never come from waiting at the threshold. It will come from crossing it.

Assisting the Mind to Evolve

To help the mind evolve, you must first understand what evolution really means in this context. It is not about discarding the mind as if it were an enemy, nor is it about bending it into submission with force or willpower. The mind is not a machine to be conquered—it is an instrument, and like any instrument, its music depends on the hands that play it. If those hands are unaware, the sound is dissonant, chaotic, a symphony of reaction and resistance. But in the hands of awareness, that same instrument becomes a channel for harmony, for clarity, for life in its highest expression.

Your mind was never designed to destroy you. It was designed to protect you. Every anxious thought, every surge of fear, every reflex to cling to what is familiar—they all began as survival codes, written in an ancient language that kept your ancestors alive. The problem is not the programming—it is the fact that you are still running codes meant for a world that no longer exists. This is what evolution asks of you: not to hate the old patterns, but to thank them for their service and then lay them to rest.

But the mind will not evolve by accident. Growth does not happen in the margins of unconscious living. It requires space. It requires silence. It requires practices that turn the gaze inward, away from the relentless noise of a world that profits from your distraction. These practices do not need to be complex. In fact, they are simple—deceptively so. A few minutes of stillness at the beginning of your day, not to escape life but to meet it fully. Breathing deeply, not because breath is trendy, but because breath is the language of the nervous system, the bridge between thought and embodiment. Reflecting before reacting, not because it looks spiritual, but because it creates the gap where choice lives. These are not small acts. They are tectonic shifts disguised as quiet moments.

And as you begin this work, be patient with yourself. The mind does not shed its old skin overnight. There will be days when you forget, days when you fall back into loops that feel like failure. They are not failures. They are part of the spiral—the upward motion of becoming, where every return to an old pattern is simply another chance to deepen your mastery. Do not measure progress by perfection; measure it by presence. By how often you return to awareness when you drift. That is the real work. That is evolution in motion.

And here is where the gentle rise begins—not as a push but as an opening: Every time you choose awareness over autopilot, you are not just changing your mind—you are reshaping your reality. Every pause, every conscious breath, every act of devotion to your own becoming is a vote for the life you long for. You may not feel the magnitude of it in the moment, but one day you will look back and see that these small, unseen acts were the architecture of your freedom.

So let this be your compass as we close this chapter: The mind you once believed was your master is not your enemy. It is your ally, waiting for you to lead. And the life you ache for is not hiding in some distant horizon—it begins here, in this choice, in this breath, in this quiet turning toward yourself with the simple but powerful intention to evolve.

Because the truth is this: you are not here to remain the same, you are here to rise—slowly, steadily, and with such depth that when you meet yourself on the other side, you will not just recognize who you have become. You will wonder how you ever lived any other way.

Chapter Two
Unconscious, Subconscious, & Conscious

> **"What you seek is seeking you."**
>
> — *Rumi*

There's a life force within you with an untapped potential ready to support your very existence in whichever way you want. This force can only be reached through mental and emotional understanding. There are many books written—and many still being written—on this topic. But what you must understand, as I explained in Chapter One, are the four principal processes: information, learning, knowledge, and understanding.

You must understand yourself. You must master yourself by understanding how your mind works, how your body responds, how your emotions move, and how your spirit lives. You cannot live this life without knowing who or what you are. For living is seeing the world through the lens of presence.

Presence is awareness. Awareness is understanding. Understanding is connection with that which you are experiencing, and experience is the mirror—the projection of our inner world. Often, you will hear that we are projectors of our own lives or that we can manifest our future. We can. And the evidence of that projection is the experience, not the world itself, but the experience of it.

Experience is the proof. The indicator. The reflection of your state of being. It mirrors the thoughts still looping inside you, the unhealed emotions from old relationships, and everything else you carry within this phenomenal machine we call a body. Experience is the heartbeat of existence; it is through experience that the life force reveals itself. But to recognize this force, you must master yourself. You must understand the very nature of what you are: an energy force. Molecular. Cellular. Tissue. Organs. Systems. An organism living within communities, ecosystems, biospheres, and beyond. You are a microcosm of the macrocosm of the multiverse. A speck of dust with problems the size of a billion dollars—when the "problem" is just a five-minute presentation or skipping a meal because you're trying to lose weight.

Above all, you are energy. An electrical vibration tuning itself into the frequencies of your understanding. You are a conscious being (mind) and an energy force (body), expressing a piece of itself as matter. As a human being, the life you are living is the result of how you look at life. The how determines the outcome. If you look at life negatively, you create resistance between you and your goals. If you look at life positively, obstacles lose power. The output of your life has no resistors when perspective shifts, when reactions shift, and when you flow.

Blame, Perspective, and the 5-Minute Pause

Often in life, we find ourselves held back by our circumstances, and we begin blaming others. We blame the system for holding us back, we say the timing isn't right, the spouse didn't support us, or no one appreciates us. It doesn't matter what formula your failure sounds like—the root cause is always the same: the failure to change your perspective.

Perspective is the great modifier. The life shifter. The invisible key to success. Until you consciously shift from perception (life is happening to me) to perspective (life is happening for me), failure will continue to knock on your door and keep you locked inside. It will keep circling until you transform how you view failure.

You see, failure is not the enemy. Failure is a moment in time filled with opportunity. Problems are situations seeking solutions. Chaos is a consolidation of information waiting for order. Your ex leaving you is an invitation to start again. Losing your job is a new beginning. The reason why you always feel like something bad "happened to you" is because of the old belief systems you refuse to challenge. Your current habits keep recycling the same experiences—like a time loop you can't escape. You keep replaying the same emotions, even when the circumstances or the people change.

So you find yourself in the same situation again and again, cursing the world: Why me? Why can't I get a break? Why do people always leave? Why me?

The truth is that life isn't happening to you. It's happening for you. But you can't see it because you're still operating from perception. Not perspective. This mindset of victimhood becomes a habit—an unconscious program that blinds you to your own power.

Understand this: life was never created to comfort your survivalist, egoic mind. On the contrary, it was created to wake you up from it. And the moment you make the decision to wake up, the game changes. When you truly see that your perception is the game shifter, you'll realize something profound: life has been inching you forward all along, providing for you, shaping you. Your next best version of yourself has been waiting inside you. Watching you while you run in circles—until that one moment when you finally shift to perspective.

Now, before we go any further, I want you to take a pause. And I mean a real pause. For the next five minutes, I want you to grab your phone, set the timer, and answer this question. Don't rush through it. Even if the answer comes quickly, stay in stillness until the timer runs out. Let silence do its work.

Here's the question:

When I experience negative emotions, how do I react—and how do I feel?

Stay there. Let it surface. And do not continue reading until the five minutes are up.

Self-Questioning & Breaking Habits

Everyone's answers will vary based on their reactions, but everyone will feel an emotion. The purpose of this exercise is simple: to introduce you to self-questioning.

Self-questioning is one of the first steps to acknowledging the conscious being within—and the first step toward breaking old habits. The egoic mind cannot question itself because it holds no self-awareness. It is reactive by design, built for one purpose: survival. Think of the egoic mind as one massive unconscious habit. And as we discussed in

Chapter One, its root emotion is fear. Its goal? To keep you reacting.

When you question yourself, you are disrupting that program. You are doubting the system the ego built to keep you safe. And in doing so, you create space. You separate yourself from what's happening outside and what's happening inside.

Imagine you are a computer. The egoic mind is the operating system—the programming. The conscious self is the software, the intelligence beyond the program. When you self-question, you become the observer, analyzing the code. You begin to identify the lines that no longer serve you—the bugs, the viruses, the patterns that have been running your life without permission. Life begins to change the moment you do this. Why? Because the code starts to shift. And this is how we begin to change our habits—not by force, but by awareness.

Through self-questioning, you take what was unconscious and make it conscious. You shine light on habits that normally slip through the cracks. And when you do this, you create the possibility of healing the emotions attached to those habits. Self-questioning is the gateway to self-realization. It is the tool your higher self uses to divorce the ego. Now, when people hear "self-questioning," they often think of self-doubt. That's not the goal here. The goal is reflection. The goal is separation—the ability to isolate thought from action, and emotion from both. The objective is to witness the thought as it arises and put it under the microscope by asking:

"How do I feel?"

"What emotions am I feeling?"

"Why did this event bother me?"

"When did I experience this before?"

When you do this, something powerful happens. You begin to reverse-engineer your mind. You isolate thought, emotion, and action as separate phenomena rather than a single identity. You begin to understand that you are not your thoughts. You are not your emotions. You are a culmination of stored experiences, compounded by time, projected by your subconscious. So when you ask, "Why do I feel this way?" you separate the feeling from the emotion—and the emotion from its origin. You trace it back to an unhealed experience hiding in the shadows, now showing up as a habit disguised as thought.

Now, I understand how complex this may sound, and I promise it will all make sense to you. But for that to happen, you need to understand the complexity of who you are, what you are, and what this conscious self truly is. The number one realization—the one that changes everything—is this: You are NOT your thoughts or your emotions.

Ludicrous, right? How can that be? If I'm not my thoughts, then who is thinking? Who is creating these thoughts?

For the next few minutes—or however long it takes you to read this section—I want you to pay close attention.

When you ask, "Who is thinking?" you are already questioning the thinking itself—and the "who" behind it. Thinking is an action, a verb. The "who" is the subject, the noun. In language, we know this as subject-verb-object. The subject is the cause of the action; the verb is the action itself.

So we can conclude this: thinking is being done by something, but that something is not the thought. It is the observer. It is the "who."

But here's where it gets interesting: what happens when the mind wanders? When you're sitting with family, trying to relax, but thoughts of work start flooding in? Or when you suddenly remember something you need to do tomorrow—without consciously deciding to think about it? How did that thought occur? How does a memory surface without your permission? If I consciously create a thought, that requires awareness. To consciously think, I must bring myself to the present and make the decision to think. So how is it that thoughts appear without conscious choice?

Here's the truth: thoughts are not being created by you—they are happening to you. They arise like clouds in the sky, formed by the evaporation of past experiences. They are the residue of everything you've lived through, condensed into patterns. What you call "mind" is simply this process: thinking happening on its own, driven by the past, running on autopilot. The ego calls it control, but it's anything but.

And this is why I say you are not your thoughts, because you can witness them. If you can watch something, then you are not it. If you can observe a thought, then you exist beyond it. You are the awareness—the silent observer—watching the movie. The main character in the movie is ego.

Do you see now? This is why you can sit in silence and notice your mind racing, why you can feel stress about something that hasn't even happened. Those thoughts are not "you." They are the echoes of unprocessed experiences still living inside you. So next time you catch yourself overthinking, remember this: thoughts are simply memories and emotions trying to replay themselves. They are data loops. They are not the truth of who you are.

To change a habit, you can't just create a new one. You must go deeper. You must find the root emotion beneath the thought, because it is the emotion that fuels the habit. This is why self-questioning matters. It reverse-engineers the process—from effect back to cause—by questioning the result (the habit) and tracing it back to the unhealed emotion that created it.

When you do this, you don't just change behavior. You transform being.

Subconsciousness

Your subconscious, in a nutshell, is the programming that started developing even before you were born.

As I mentioned earlier in Chapter Two, genetics plays a role not only in physical characteristics but in temperaments and tendencies. Through evolution, genetic mechanisms allowed us to pass down survival-based behaviors—and this is why species, including us, have endured for thousands of years.

What I find fascinating is how this shows up in our families, how we all seem to have relatives who share the same laughter, the same walk, even the same emotional triggers and tempers. The subconscious isn't just your current programming—it's a living archive of ancestral patterns.

Think about it: your subconscious holds both the good and the bad, the nurturing and the traumatic, the encouragement and the neglect. It stores every experience you've had and many you never lived personally but inherited through generations. We often think of the subconscious as something operating only in the present moment, like a hidden mental state. But in truth, your subconscious is a tapestry woven from the threads of your entire lineage and your own life.

I want you to imagine the subconscious as a substitute teacher—a stand-in for the real teacher, which is consciousness. The substitute walks into the classroom with their own rules, personality, and assumptions. It doesn't teach from the original curriculum. It improvises based on memory, past experiences, and its interpretation of authority.

Now imagine that substitute teacher living inside you—making decisions, reacting to life, running the show. It believes it's in control. It believes it is you. And you believe it too.

But here's the paradox: most of your decisions—what you call "free will"—aren't truly free. They're pre-scripted by this substitute. They've been influenced, shaped, and often predetermined by experiences you've had and by ancestral memories you didn't even know were part of your story. And so you live life thinking you're the captain of your ship, unaware that the map, the compass, and even the destination was programmed long before you took the wheel. This is why we need to dismantle the illusion of control. Not to disempower you—but to wake you up. Because here's the truth: you are not the programming. You are the consciousness capable of rewriting it.

Thinking this way changes everything. It forces you to see that your thoughts are not random. They're patterns. Your habits are not accidental. They're inherited. Even your beliefs—the ones you defend so passionately—were passed down to you like a family heirloom you never questioned. This is why people wake up at the same time every day, scroll their phones, brush their teeth, drink coffee, go to work or school, take breaks at predictable times, and end their day in front of a screen. It's why their emotional reactions follow the same grooves day after day, year after year. Thoughts become automated. Actions become ritual. Life becomes a cycle—an unconscious repetition masquerading as freedom.

And here's the thing: your subconscious is not your enemy. It's not trying to ruin you. It was designed to protect you. It has kept you alive, responded in emergencies, and pulled you out of danger. When you swerved just in time to avoid a car accident? That was your subconscious. When you instinctively grabbed something as you slipped? That was your subconscious, too. It knows every survival mechanism. It remembers every lesson—yours and your ancestors'. It's an energy field of stored experiences encoded in your nervous system, ready to act in a millisecond.

But here's the catch: the same system that saves your life in crisis is the one that sabotages your growth in peace. Because its purpose is not to make you thrive—it's to make you survive.

To transcend this, you don't kill the subconscious. You don't destroy the substitute teacher. You teach it. You lead it. You reprogram it with awareness.

And that begins with understanding that you are not your thoughts, not your habits, and not the patterns passed down to you. You are the consciousness observing all of it—and you have the power to change the script.

Consciousness

When I speak about consciousness, people often assume it simply means being awake. They think of it as the opposite of sleep, a binary state of awareness versus unconsciousness. But what I am referring to goes far beyond this basic interpretation. When you become conscious in the way I am describing, something shifts so profoundly that people often call it awakening. And the language is fitting because it feels as if you've awakened from a dream you didn't know you were in—a dream you once called reality.

In my own journey, awakening was not something I studied or prepared for. It was not a choice I made. It was an event that erupted in my life like a storm, unannounced and unstoppable. I stepped into my hero's journey blindfolded, without a map, without a clue about what was happening to me mentally, emotionally, or physically. Words like *dark night of the soul*, *psychosomatic healing*, *breathwork*, *panic attacks*, and *awakening* were foreign to me at the time. And yet, they became my vocabulary as I walked through six months of relentless panic attacks, wondering if I was dying, only to discover that what was happening was not death—it was rebirth.

My awakening wasn't something beautiful and serene, at least not in the beginning. It was chaos. It was terror. It was the collapse of everything I believed I was. But as painful as it was, I can tell you now—it was the greatest gift life could have ever given me. This is what I want you to understand: consciousness is not learned through books or acquired through memorization. It is not intellectual. Consciousness is lived. It is felt. It is experienced as a complete reorientation of self. When you begin to awaken, you begin to see everything differently—not because the world changed, but because *you* did. Awakening forces you to revisit places within you that you've avoided for years—the corners filled with shame, pain, and old trauma. It drags everything into the light, whether you are ready or not. This is why I say awakening is not for the faint of heart. It requires surrender. It demands the letting go of attachments, identities, and illusions you've clung to for a lifetime. And yet, once you pass through this fire, everything changes. You begin to feel again—not just surface feelings, but the depth of existence itself. You develop a new sensitivity to life, a new clarity that cannot be undone.

Consciousness is not a process. It is not a system. It is not a step-by-step method. It is a collapse of time and space into a singular point of awareness where everything just *is*. When you awaken, problems as you once knew them lose their weight. They no longer dominate your life because you see through them. You see them for what they are: illusions born from the ego's need for control.

Imagine thinking about a person who once caused you pain. Before awakening, that thought triggers a storm—anger, resentment, grief. After awakening, that same memory carries no charge. It loses its energy the moment you truly see it for what it is: a past event that only exists now as thought. This is the power of consciousness. It transforms pain into presence. It transmutes fear into freedom. It elevates you beyond the confines of ego and mind into a state where you witness everything without being enslaved by it.

And this is why I tell you: consciousness is beyond thought. It is beyond mind. It is the witness to both. When you live from this place, life becomes fluid. You become less of a doer and more of a being. You stop reacting and start existing in harmony with what is. Consciousness is not something you chase. It is what remains when the noise inside you falls silent.

Unconsciousness

What I call unconsciousness is the state of being unaware of your thoughts and emotions—a state where life is happening, but you are not truly present for it. An unconscious person is easily influenced, not just by their own thoughts, but by external noise: the news, social media, gossip from the neighbor, the endless chatter of a world that thrives on distraction.

Being unconscious is dangerous because it makes you vulnerable to manipulation by others and by your own mind. Sadly, much of the world today lives in this state, unaware, moving through life like sleepwalkers, and this is why I write these words—not to offend, but to awaken.

Let me ask you: have you ever lost your temper and said something you wish you could take back? Have you ever felt guilt for something you should have done but didn't, or for words you spoke that wounded someone? Have you ever wondered why so many people are drowning in debt, trapped in addiction, numbing themselves with substances, binge-watching screens, and consuming information that adds no value to their lives? Why are children today addicted to social media before they even understand who they are?

Unconsciousness explains it all.

When you are unconscious, your actions feel automatic because they are. They happen in tandem with your thoughts and emotions—almost like a reflex. And here's the strangest part: when you are unconscious, it feels normal. It feels like you are right. It feels like this is just who you are.

Living unconsciously is like being sick with an illness that has no symptoms—or so you think. It's like having a cold your whole life and believing that's how breathing is supposed to feel. Chaos becomes your normal. Drama feels like home. And because it feels familiar, you never question it. You begin to identify with the narrative your mind keeps writing: that you are the victim, that life is unfair, that nothing ever works out for you. And because you believe these stories, they become the script you live by.

Unconsciousness is hypnosis—the kind that doesn't need a swinging watch because your mind has become the hypnotist. You are under its spell, living out patterns from the past and calling it "me."

And here's what makes it more dangerous: when you are unconscious, you will defend this state as truth. You will insist that the problem is never you—it's always someone else. You will point fingers, assign blame, and reject anyone who challenges your perspective. Your ego becomes the silent author of your life, and you never question its authority. It writes your failures. It dictates your reactions. It convinces you that you are in control when, in reality, you're on autopilot, acting out scenes from an old script you didn't even write. Unconsciousness feels like freedom because you don't feel the weight of awareness—but it is the heaviest chain you will ever wear.

And here's the final paradox: being unconscious is still a state of consciousness. It's just the lowest frequency of it. It's consciousness asleep, dreaming it's awake. And in that dream, you will keep repeating the same loops until something inside you finally says, *Enough*.

When that moment comes—and it will—you will see that every problem, every failure, every broken relationship, every sleepless night was life calling you home. And home is awareness. Home is consciousness. Home is you.

Chapter Three
Ego

> **"Until you make the unconscious conscious, it will direct your life and you will call it fate."**
>
> — Carl Jung

At the beginning of this book, I explained how, in August 2022, I suffered a huge panic attack that almost cost me my life. It was the moment when all hell broke loose—when Pandora's box opened, forcing my transformation—and I made the decision to go on this journey alone, without any medication or psychological assistance.

As I mentioned earlier, ego is nothing more than an accumulation of unprocessed experiences seeking to be experienced because, at some point, we suppressed them, ignored them, or blamed someone else to avoid feeling. Ego is also your natural survival instinct, designed to react in any given moment based on genetic coding passed down from your ancestors. In essence, the ego is the result of unprocessed energies still within the body.

The key to understanding the ego and mind is this: you are not the sum of your experiences, but the awareness behind them. You are something separate from the experience itself. Think about it this way: in order to experience a strawberry, there must be a subject and an object. If you have a thought that creates an emotion, remember—you cannot be that thought. What sets you apart, and connects you at the same time, is the experience itself. It is the relation between subject and object. The experience is what makes it feel real, and yet the experience is not you.

That's why when we express emotions, we say things like, *"I feel happy"* or *"I feel sad."* When we ask someone close to us how they are doing, we ask, *"How do you feel?"* The experience fools us into believing we are what we feel or think. Let me explain with a real example I had to overcome.

In August 2022, in the middle of a panic attack, I paced around my home, consumed by fear—fear of dying, fear of harming myself. I feared my rapid breathing. I feared the pounding of my heart, the dizziness, the fatigue overwhelming my body. I was a complete mess, hoping these symptoms would disappear. But after weeks of experiencing them nonstop, the thought of death seemed like a better escape, and my mind began to develop suicidal thoughts.

I never consciously wanted to die. In fact, I was terrified of dying and desperately wanted to live. But at that time, the thought of living didn't even register. The single ray of light in that dark tunnel was my struggle to make sense of what was happening to me, both in body and in mind. Physically, I went to the doctors and got myself checked out. *"Mr. Lopez, you are healthy,"* the doctor said. All of my bloodwork came back normal. If anything, during this time, I actually improved my cholesterol, which had been creeping upward for the first time in my life. I did every test—sleep apnea study, thorough heart checkups, endless bloodwork. Even the top VA cardiologist examined my heart. My liver, kidneys, thyroid—all good.

I did my due diligence, and every time, the results came back normal. Yet, no matter what the doctors said, I was always feeling something. There was pain in my chest, sometimes pain in my arms, and pain in different areas. What was interesting was how the pains would appear for a day, maybe weeks, and then dissolve—only to appear somewhere else. It was almost like my body was playing games with me. The pains were random. Unexpected.

I realized that whenever something hurt, I became a hypochondriac, rushing to the ER for help. I began to think I had cancer. That something severe was hiding under my skin. Any pain, no matter how small, no matter what part of my body—it must be cancer. Or something worse. But the reality was simple: mentally, I was a complete mess, and my survival instincts were at 300% alert. Something inside me had woken up, and I became hyper-aware of every heartbeat.

My mind was winning this battle, but I hadn't connected the dots yet. My mind questioned every symptom in my body. Every breath. Every heartbeat. The taste in my mouth. The look in my eyes. Everything became a source of doubt. My ego was making me overthink and start creating visions that I now call "movie trailers" in my mind.

I know how silly this may sound, but it's important to pause here. This is one dimension of ego-mind you must understand. It is dynamic, complex, and powerful. So please pay close attention because these trailers almost cost me my life.

Movie Trailers

The movie trailers I began to develop in my head were strange, and at first, I could not understand what was happening. They came uninvited, and they were vivid, emotional, and overwhelming. Let me explain what these "movie trailers" looked like.

Imagine closing your eyes and reliving a positive memory from childhood—a birthday party, a time when someone surprised you with kindness. If you focus deeply on that memory, you not only see it but feel the emotions attached to it. Now, replace that memory with something you have never actually lived, yet it feels real. It floods you with sensations you do not want to experience. That is what was happening to me.

The first movie trailer was the idea that I had cancer. I could see myself lying in a hospital bed surrounded by my loved ones, saying goodbye. It felt so real, I could smell the room and hear the machines beeping. I had never lived this before, yet my mind made it real enough to convince me. At first, I fought these visions, running from them as fast as I could—mentally, emotionally, spiritually—because they terrified me.

One day, I called my sister and told her what was happening. She said something that would change everything: *"Why don't you just die?"*

At first, I was shocked. *"What do you mean, die?"* I asked. *"Lay down,"* she said. *"Take yourself to that movie you keep fighting. Experience it. Feel it. See what happens."*

Her words sounded absurd, but my mind was already consumed 24/7 by this impending fear of death. It had gotten so bad that I made sure my life insurance was in order and my beneficiaries knew exactly who would receive what. I even wrote letters to my loved ones saying goodbye.

That day, after my sister's suggestion, I decided to try. I laid down on the couch, closed my eyes, and pressed play. No popcorn. No soda. Only terror. Alone.

Pixel by pixel, frame by frame, second by second, I surrendered to it, and the movie trailer converted into a real live movie. My body was now in the movie. I saw my daughters' faces as I lay in that hospital bed, knowing I would never see them again. I cried both in the vision and in real life, sobbing so hard my body shook. I moved from my daughters to my parents, saying, *"Thank you for loving me and taking care of me,"* then to my sisters. I thanked them all and cried until my body ached.

The emotions were excruciating, the fear unbearable, and yet something within me was shifting. What were images before they became a real-life experience? I don't want to call it an out-of-body experience, but it felt like another dimension within my own. I could feel the bed beneath me, I could see the walls, and the faces of everyone were so clear. In retrospect, it was as if this experience was designed for me—to hold space for my transmutation.

When the experience ended, I opened my eyes. At first, I felt almost the same, but as the day went on, the calm began to grow. The movie trailer didn't return that night. When it did try to come back, I made space for it. I sat with it. No more running. I learned that the more I faced these fears, the weaker they became. Within a week, I had seen this movie three or four times. Each time, the intensity lessened, and a strange peace began to grow.

What did I learn? That the ego and mind are not enemies, but survival programs fighting to keep themselves alive—even if it costs you your peace. Ego controls your habits, thoughts, and emotions. It will fight change with everything it has because it only knows one way: the old way. It knows how to crash your nervous system, flood you with cortisol, and activate your sympathetic response because that's how it makes you feel alive.

But here's the truth: you are not your ego. You are the awareness that observes it. Ego death, as many call it, isn't about killing the ego. It's about separating from it—becoming so aware that ego can no longer control the trajectory of your life.

Biology

Biology is one of the prism's sides to healing and a fundamental tool for coexisting in this reality we call life. To truly understand the human experience, we must develop a deep interest in this science, because within it lies the key to comprehending the mind's faculties and the body's profound impact on them. The body is a masterpiece of systems—each one a symphony—managing blood circulation, body temperature, heartbeats, breathing, cell regeneration, and more.

Yet one system stands above the rest in its influence: the autonomic nervous system. From birth, we are equipped with an advanced internal network capable of running on autopilot, managing countless processes without a single conscious command. Your heart beats approximately 100,000 times a day, pumping nearly 2,000 gallons of blood through your veins. Your lungs breathe in oxygen and expel carbon dioxide about 22,000 times every single day. Over the span of a lifetime, your heart will beat an average of 2.5 billion times, pumping millions of gallons of blood—silent, precise, unwavering.

Pause for a moment and think about that. If these numbers didn't make you skip a heartbeat or take a deep breath, they should. How can we continue living our lives without acknowledging the most sophisticated piece of machinery that allows us to experience this existence? Your biology is no accident. If anything, it demands reverence—a level of respect reserved for miracles.

But science doesn't stop there. When you were born, you were blasted into this reality carrying billions of neurons coded with ancestral genetics. These neural blueprints determined everything from your skin tone and eye color to your height, weight, gender, and even predispositions for certain health conditions. They even shaped aspects of your personality—the quirks and temperaments that make you "you." Think about those moments when family members say, *"You act just like your grandfather"*—they're not wrong. Much of who you are is a genetic echo of those who came before.

And it's not just the good stuff that gets passed down. Along with beauty marks and dimples come medical conditions, mental health vulnerabilities, and habits carried through generations. But here's the truth you need to tattoo on your mind: **you have the power to change those inherited scripts.** You are not doomed to live by genetic default. You don't have to agree with the false narrative that your biology is your destiny.

This body—the most advanced machine in this space-time reality—is not just a collection of organs and cells. It's a living interface between ego and awareness, between consciousness and experience. And its complexity demands more than casual curiosity. Unless you take time to study it, to really understand how it works, you will never fully grasp the depth of its connection to your thoughts, emotions, and feelings. The nervous system, in particular, is the bridge that links what you think to what you feel—and ultimately, to what you become.

In the next chapters, we'll explore the science of the body to uncover not just what you are, but who you are. And by the time you say, *"I feel happy,"* you'll know exactly why.

Let's start with a simple exercise. Go back over the last 15 minutes, the past hour, your day, even your week. Ask yourself: What did I eat? Who did I spend time with? Where was I? What did I do—did I work out, run, or push through a hard day? What time of day is it? And then ask the bigger question: Why do I feel the way I feel right now?

You see, many of us believe happiness is just a state of being, but it's not. Happiness is the byproduct of choices—the food you eat, the people you allow into your space, the habits you maintain, the conversations you entertain, and the environments you place yourself in. Happiness is the result of discipline and intention. It's the accumulation of small decisions repeated over time, built into the muscle memory of your life until it becomes second nature.

And yet, happiness alone isn't enough. There's another layer to this—a level of awareness that explains the why behind what you feel. Yes, exercise can pull you out of depression, but if you don't pair that movement with reflection, you'll miss the bigger picture: your emotions are biochemical, but they are also deeply tied to thought and consciousness. Biologically, your moods are influenced by chemical agents like dopamine, serotonin, norepinephrine, oxytocin, cortisol, and others. They shape your feelings, but they do not dictate your emotions. Emotions are interwoven with your thoughts, and your thoughts reflect your awareness.

We've all heard the idea that low serotonin is to blame for depression, and while serotonin does play a role, it isn't the root cause. The choices we make in life are. Serotonin doesn't decide who you love, what you fear, or which dreams you pursue—it simply reacts to the narrative you live by. So when you say, *"I feel happy,"* what you're really saying is, *"I engaged in behaviors that spiked my dopamine or serotonin and created a temporary chemical experience."*

Your life is a perfect mirror of your inner world. The point of this chapter is to ignite your curiosity—to remind you that you're not just existing. You're experiencing, and the vehicle allowing this experience is your body. If you learn to understand it, to respect it, and to partner with it, you'll unlock one of the greatest keys to your evolution.

But here's the paradox: for all its brilliance, the body didn't come with an instruction manual. Unlike the Ikea furniture that came with an instruction manual, this machine arrived without a guidebook. Instead, you were handed a set of generational blueprints, some of which you didn't ask for, encoded with ancestral imprints that echo as feelings and emotions in your nervous system. These signals—whether joyful or painful—are invitations. They are calls to awareness.

The body is both ancient and advanced, mechanical and mystical, a paradox of biology and spirit. And every single process, every spark of the nervous system, every chemical surge exists for one reason: to give meaning to your experience. What is an experience without feeling? A feeling without an emotion? An emotion without meaning? Everything in you is connected. Everything in life leads back to one root: **emotion.**

Force & Nervous System

The nervous system is a masterpiece—an intricate network of electrical impulses firing at incredible speed, carrying messages that decide whether you sip a warm cup of coffee in peace or snap into fight, flight, or freeze mode at the sound of a gunshot. It's astonishing how quickly we can respond to danger without conscious thought, almost as if there is an unseen intelligence guiding us. But there's nothing mystical about this—science calls it survival.

Your central nervous system is your command center, made up of the brain, spinal cord, and a vast network of nerves. The brain processes information, orchestrates physical movement, and regulates emotions. The spinal cord is the superhighway of signals between the three-pound universe inside your skull and the rest of your body. And the nerves—those root-like fibers—carry electrical impulses that control every sensation, every reflex, every involuntary act keeping you alive.

Think about this: billions of neurological connections firing every second without a single conscious effort from you. It is this quiet, relentless intelligence that leaves me in awe. Most people never stop to marvel at this system because life is loud and demanding, but the truth is, when you silence the noise, you can feel it—you can even hear it. The steady thump of your heart, the rhythm of your breath. This orchestra of biology plays for you every day from sunrise to sunset, and yet most of us never say, *"Thank you, body."*

We ignore it until it malfunctions. Until the diagnosis comes. Until the body whispers with symptoms we brushed off, then screams when we keep ignoring it. Suddenly, the life we thought was so important—the job, the car, the endless obligations—shrinks to nothing in the shadow of one desperate wish: to get better. We bargain with life for what we once took for granted.

Why wait for that moment? Why not honor this miracle now? Why not hold reverence for your health while you still have it? Five minutes of gratitude for your body can transform the way you experience life. But here's the paradox: most of us don't stop until our bodies force us to. I know, because I learned this lesson the hard way.

When I became ill and found myself in and out of emergency rooms, nothing else mattered. Not the house. Not the job. Not the bills. All I wanted was to live. That experience shattered my illusions and uncovered a powerful truth: within us lies a force that can either build us up or tear us down. A force that can quietly sustain you or violently bring you to your knees. For months, I wrestled with this power, and what I discovered changed my life forever.

This force—the one humming inside you at this very moment—does not need your permission to act. It is faithful, disciplined, and relentless. It works for you without complaint, without rest. But it is not passive. If you abuse it long enough, it will revolt. It will override your stubborn will and seize control in ways you will not enjoy. It will somatically choke you into submission, forcing you to change or perish.

When my sympathetic nervous system activated, it was like the Power Rangers screaming, *"It's morphin' time!"* Except there was no hero moment—only panic, chaos, and months of hell. That activation manifested as a severe panic attack that didn't last minutes or hours but nearly six months. Six months of psychological torture. Six months of thinking I was dying every single day.

My body slammed the brakes on my life and dragged me to a full stop. The physical symptoms were unbearable. Thoughts of death on repeat. Anxiety spiking into full-blown terror. Depression clawing at my mind. My heart racing out of control. Numbness creeping into my face and limbs. Trouble breathing so severe that every inhale felt like a desperate act of survival. Nights spent gasping for air as if my body forgot how to breathe.

I became hyper-aware of every function. Every breath felt manual, as if my autonomic nervous system threw its hands up and said, *"Fine, you take over since you don't want to listen."* Do you know what it's like to think about every single breath you take for months? To live sunrise to sunset in a constant state of alarm? It was madness. Sometimes I would wake up choking, certain I had stopped breathing. Other times, I couldn't pull enough air into my lungs no matter how hard I tried—though somehow, I always self-regulated.

Doctors ran every test imaginable—heart, lungs, thyroid, blood panels, scans. Every result came back the same: *"Mr. Lopez, you're fine."* But I didn't feel fine. I felt like I was dying from the inside out. That contradiction drove me deeper into research—neuroscience, biology, psychology, spirituality. I needed answers because my body was screaming a language I didn't yet understand.

What I learned became the foundation of my transformation. The parasympathetic nervous system is your homeostasis—your calm, balanced state of being. The sympathetic system? That's your fight-or-flight command center, and when it flips on for too long, it will burn your body to the ground. Short bursts of stress can make you stronger—that's called *hormesis*, and science loves this word—but chronic stress is a slow poison. It inflames your body, hijacks your hormones, and warps your mind.

Looking back, I see it clearly now. My nervous system wasn't broken. It was doing its job—loudly, violently, but with perfect precision. It was trying to save me from a life I could no longer live. The panic wasn't punishment; it was a warning, a red siren screaming: *"Change or die."*

And here's the truth that most people miss: your life mirrors your nervous system. If you are living in chaos, stress, and denial, your body will reflect it until you wake up. What was happening outside of me was happening inside of me. My body was the battlefield where old habits went to die.

The lesson? This force within you—the intelligence behind every heartbeat, every breath—is not here to destroy you. It's here to push you toward your highest self. But if you ignore it, it will use pain as its loudest teacher.

You can study all the sciences in the world—and I recommend you do—but nothing will transform your life until you evolve your consciousness. Because the nervous system, as magical as it is, is still a servant. The master is awareness. Awareness turns pain into perspective. It takes fear and transmutes it into fuel. And that is where true power begins.

Thoughts vs. Thinking

Can you imagine a consciousness that simply is—existing without the constant noise of thought? A state of pure being, without the need for senses, without the endless interpretations of reality? Picture this: no external world pulling at you, no inner storm twisting your emotions. Experience and existence finally separated, like two worlds drawn apart by their own nature.

What would remain? Awareness—raw, unshaped, unbroken. A presence that doesn't need a name because it is the name.

In that state, you begin to see that what you call *being angry* or *being happy, being anxious* or *being depressed,* are not permanent truths. They are transient states—passing clouds across the vast sky of consciousness. They do not define you. They visit you, move through you, and dissolve. But they are not you.

This is the power of distinguishing between thoughts and thinking. A thought is an image, an impulse, an echo of memory. Thinking is the act of engaging with it—feeding it attention, giving it shape and weight. Thinking is where we take the passing cloud and decide to build a house under it.

The goal is not to destroy thought—you can't. The goal is to stop drowning in it. To realize that you can observe the thought without becoming it. When you understand this, something radical happens: you gain the ability to interrupt patterns that once ran your life on autopilot.

Because here's the truth: most of what you feel is not caused by reality but by the thoughts you keep rehearsing about reality. That loop becomes your identity. Break the loop, and you begin to see the paradox: you were never your anger, your anxiety, your sadness—you were always the one watching.

This is where transmutation begins—where you take the raw energy of thought and elevate it into something higher. Not by resisting it, but by understanding it. Because what you understand, you can transcend.

Why Become Conscious

Becoming consciously aware is the greatest gift the universe offers those willing to answer the call. And yet, that call often comes disguised as chaos—divorce, loss, financial collapse, betrayal, illness. These events rip the calm from your life and replace it with storms so violent they shake the ground you stand on. That's how it was for me.

I didn't walk into awakening through candlelight and mantras. I crawled into it through broken glass. By the time I realized I was in the rabbit hole, my life was already in pieces—marriage ending, finances wrecked, faith cracked open like a fault line. And yet, something inside me kept whispering, *"Keep going. There's more."*

I didn't know where the edge led, but I was ready to leap. I was prepared to lose everything—even myself—because some part of me knew this wasn't the end. It was the beginning of becoming.

Here's what most people don't understand: the path to consciousness rarely starts with clarity. It starts in the dark. Conscious awareness doesn't exist at first because, if it did, there wouldn't be a path to walk. You begin blind, fumbling, colliding with your own shadows. And that's the point. Awareness is not a noun—it's a verb. It's a process of illumination, one painful inch at a time.

At first, the shift is almost imperceptible. A flicker of light in a cave you thought was endless. But then something changes—you start to notice patterns. You begin to separate yourself from the storm inside your head. You go from perception to perspective, from *"life is happening to me"* to *"life is happening for me."*

This shift is everything. It doesn't erase pain, but it gives pain a purpose. Suddenly, the obstacles that felt like punishment start looking like training. The gym makes sense when your muscles burn because you know growth is happening. The same principle applies to life: you grow stronger through resistance.

The path to awakening feels brutal because it dismantles the illusions you built your life on. It strips away comfort, tears down false identities, and leaves you naked with yourself. That is why so few people choose it—and why those who do become unshakable.

Awakening is like basic training for the soul—except there's no drill sergeant, no schedule, no end date. The obstacles are custom-designed by your own consciousness: your trauma, your habits, your fears. And here's the paradox—they were never here to break you. They were here to reveal you.

When you finally embrace this, the game changes. Choices become clear. Decisions stop feeling like battles. You stop drowning in thought because you finally know who's swimming.

And the reward? Not medals or certificates. The prize for walking this path is freedom—the kind that cannot be taken, because it doesn't come from outside you. It's the freedom of knowing that no storm can shake what you've anchored inside.

Closing the Loop

Everything in life—ego, biology, the nervous system—is a mirror of the same universal principle: **energy seeking balance**. The ego fights to keep old patterns alive because its only mission is survival. Biology reacts to the environments you choose—physical and mental—and speaks in the language of symptoms. The nervous system? It's the messenger, translating your internal chaos into physical reality. None of these forces are against you. They're for you. They are guides, not enemies.

The problem is that we live as if we are these forces. We believe we are our thoughts, our emotions, our pain. We identify with the messenger and miss the message. The truth? **You are none of these things.** You are the awareness observing them—the still point beneath the storm, the presence behind the pulse. Becoming conscious is not about becoming perfect. It's about becoming aware enough to stop living as a hostage to your biology and begin living as the author of your existence. It's about recognizing that every thought is a seed, every emotion a signal, and every reaction a chance to evolve.

This is where the shift begins—from autopilot to intention, from reacting to creating, from surviving to living. But awareness isn't handed to you. It's earned in the trenches of experience. It's carved out in the nights you can't sleep, the mornings you don't think you'll make it, the moments you want to quit but don't.

Because one day, without fanfare, you wake up and realize the truth: **the storm didn't come to destroy you—it came to reveal you.**

And that realization is the door to the next chapter: **how we heal, transmute, and rise beyond the patterns that once defined us.**

Chapter Four
Solitude

> **"You must lose yourself to find yourself."**
>
> — *Unknown*

Five monkeys were placed in a large cage, and high at the top, beyond their reach, hung a bunch of bananas. Beneath the bananas was a ladder. The monkeys saw the fruit, and one began to climb, only to be sprayed with cold water by the experimenter, who then turned the hose on the others until all five were wet, cold, and confused. After some time, another monkey tried to climb, tempted by the bananas, and again the punishment came—cold water for him and the entire group. When a third attempted the climb, the others, desperate to avoid the spray, dragged him down and beat him.

Then, one of the original monkeys was removed and replaced with a new one. The newcomer spotted the bananas and naturally began to climb. Immediately, the other monkeys pulled him down and beat him without hesitation. Here's where it gets interesting: as more of the original monkeys were replaced, the same behavior continued. Even monkeys that had never been sprayed with cold water joined in the beatings. Eventually, none of the original monkeys remained, yet every time a newcomer tried to climb the ladder, the others attacked. None of them knew why. They just knew: "This is how it's done." The experiment revealed something disturbing: behavior, once conditioned, can outlive its cause.

The thoughts that developed after reading this experiment… shook me.

So now ask yourself these questions: what behaviors, mental mindsets, or belief systems has society influenced upon you without your knowing? Have you been conditioned in ways you never questioned? Have you been a victim of the monkey experiment? And even more troubling, have you ever victimized someone else without conscious intent?

You see, when I began my healing and came across this experiment, it was like being cornered by a sword, pressed against the wall, leaving me with no option but to self-question every dimension of who I was. From the root of causality to the rippling, reciprocating effects of every decision I had ever made. This new understanding unearthed forty years of unconscious conditioning and widened the aperture of my perception—it birthed perspective. When I finally shifted from perception to perspective—or in simpler words, from life happening to me to life happening for me—I began to question absolutely everything. I began to question everything, my ancestral beliefs, my traditions, my culture, and the unhealed traumas carried by generations before me. Were they victims too? Did they, in their own unconsciousness, become the victimizers of others?

I questioned my childhood, not simply asking whether it was good or bad, but wondering which events influenced me, which experiences molded my sense of self. What potential traumas shaped the entire course of my life? These were the questions I faced and answered in my solitude. I realized then that no manual for life existed—and maybe that was the point. Perhaps the journey of self-inquiry is what it means to truly live.

Solitude gave me the space to think for myself, to process the roots of my being, and to unlearn the life I had been practicing unconsciously. It taught me that the work wasn't about answers—it was about becoming conscious. It was about asking questions that cut through the noise of conditioning. Questions that forced me to look inward rather than outward.

The answers, over time, became less important than the questions themselves. With every new question, something unexpected happened: I didn't gain more information—I gained self-awareness. And in that self-awareness, I discovered a new kind of intelligence, one that can't be measured by the five senses, only felt through presence.

Living in solitude taught me a truth I hadn't expected: I had been deeply disconnected from myself. My life had been a huge reciprocating effect of everything I had ever known, everyone who ever influenced me, from my decision to join the military, to my religious preferences, to my taste in food, my ideas about success, love, money, and relationships. Everything I thought was "me" was, in reality, borrowed. And the most troubling question emerged: whose life am I really living? My parents' dreams? My ancestors' hopes? Am I living through the lens of trauma? And if so, what experiences have I unknowingly excluded from my existence because of it?

In solitude, I came to terms with everything—my passions, my love, my bliss, but also my disagreements, my dislikes, my hate, my biases. I discovered writing as my gift, supported by deep thinking, relentless curiosity, and what I can only call the whisper of higher consciousness. In solitude, I forgave myself and reconciled old emotional memories. I granted myself permission to become who I was, who I am—the self who had hidden behind fear like a scared child lost in the forest.

The most beautiful moment was a microsecond of eternity: when I looked at the shadow of myself with glossy eyes, full of humility, love, peace, and acceptance of who I was in the present. And in that sacred instant, an unimaginable, wordless, universal love surged through me—a love so pure it cannot be comprehended by the five senses but only by an intelligence beyond them.

So you see, solitude wasn't loneliness—it was liberation. It allowed me to process my life, revisit my past, and address every trauma. Only then could I start living my own life. Going into solitude was, and still is, one of the most profound experiences of my existence. I needed that space to expand my consciousness so that I could share this story with you. Today marks several years since my divorce, and when I reflect on my initial fears—fear of being alone, fear of breaking apart a life I had built—I marvel at what came after. I discovered a wholeness within myself that taught me something essential: being alone is not the same as being lonely.

I look at my life now and realize how much quality time I share with my kids, how much more present I am, how my worries have dissolved into trust. I was able to quit my job, to walk away from everything that was no longer aligned—and somehow, everything worked itself out. Now, I'm not saying divorce is the answer for everyone, but solitude… solitude gives you a once-in-a-lifetime opportunity to reflect, to reconcile your thoughts and emotions, and to realize how much noise we create just to avoid the truth of our own souls.

In solitude, I faced the deepest questions: Why do I feel the need to be with someone? Why can't I be alone and happy? Why do I feel empty without someone to share my life with? Was it a need to love—or to be loved? What is love? One question led to another until the ground beneath my feet gave way and I fell into the void of my own being. And in that fall, I realized this: to live fully, I had to resolve every emotion in every memory, through self-experience.

I learned that today is all that matters, that if yesterday repeats itself today, it signals something unhealed within me. I learned to embrace every emotion that surfaced—to feel it fully, whether it was anger, grief, anxiety, or depression—without resistance, until it passed through me. That's why living alone in my apartment after the divorce became a vital part of my recovery. Without it, I would have never fully understood the energy within me. I needed to heal. I needed to elevate my consciousness before awakening to my higher self—an awareness untouched by time and space, a force as vast as the multiverse.

While I wish I could share everything I discovered in that space, some truths defy explanation because our senses are too limited. These truths require a higher consciousness, a level of awareness accessible to anyone willing to look inward. But in the beginning, I wasn't ready. When the bottom broke beneath me, I felt unprepared. I didn't understand what was happening. My mind was in chaos, my emotions a storm, and yet, in the midst of that chaos, something sacred was emerging: a higher self-awakening.

As I wrestled with PTSD, childhood trauma, and the reality of who I was and who I had not become, I experienced every polarity—sadness and joy, fear and love, chaos and harmony—until, finally, peace. Slowly, I began to separate my mind and body from what I truly was. Understanding became something more than knowledge—it became consciousness. And in that shift, I discovered a new dimension of myself, one beyond definitions, beyond words, beyond the illusion of permanence.

Mind–Memory

Being conditioned for a lifetime is an awkward experience, but daring not to experiment with the truth of who you are is a subconscious sin. The mind, with its infinite thoughts and multi-realities, is a talented machine built for survival—even if that survival means terrorizing its own home. It is a peculiar force with its own complexities, characteristics, and intentions. Its ultimate goal is simple: to keep you alive, to avoid death at all costs. But what does it really mean for the mind to avoid death? How does this instinct manifest itself? Is it good—or is it bad?

Even as I ask that question, I find it fascinating how easily we accept assumptions. Why do we assume death is bad? Why is it that the very thought of death creates tension in the mind and body? The answer is conditioning. We have been programmed to fear death since birth, and because of that conditioning, we create biases that cloud the truth. And when truth is hidden, life dissolves into an endless cycle of illusions, shadows mistaken for reality.

So here lies the problem: you think you are your mind. You think you are your thoughts. You think every idea that crosses your mental screen is yours. You live through thought, crediting the mind for every success and blaming the world for every failure. Yet when it comes time for the mind to take responsibility, it vanishes, because the mind is not who you are—it is an independent system serving one purpose: survival. That is why we call it egoistic.

The mind is a forward-action machine. It operates like a well-trained soldier, always planning the next move, always preparing for the next threat. In many ways, it is like an AI program—created to manage and predict when the real teacher, the conscious self, falls asleep. The mind is good and bad. Good because it has kept you alive; bad because it hijacks your freedom and blinds you to truth by making you think, and think, and think some more. Because when the mind is thinking, it is alive; it has purpose. When the mind is silent, it becomes useless. And when the mind becomes useless, it loses control—and that terrifies it.

But here is the deeper truth: when the mind loses control, the truth reveals itself. And that truth is you. The real you—the one you have felt in fleeting moments of creative flow, in childhood wonder, in the spaces where you lose track of time. The version of you that does not need to think in order to live. The you that writes without forcing words, that paints without planning every stroke, that runs not for reward but for the sheer freedom of motion. The pure self—the artist, the thinker, the athlete, the creator—does not rely on the mind to think or to do. It simply expresses.

This self flows like a river, merging imagination with action, and creates not through calculation but through being. It is a force beyond thought—a living symbiosis that the mind often interrupts with its noise. But let's be clear: the mind is not entirely useless. It has a role. It has always had a role. Its purpose, however, must now be determined by you—the conscious self, the teacher awakened to reclaim the captaincy of its own ship. This is why we say, "awaken."

Now let me ask you: have you ever wondered why we had to label the mind? Why did we give it a name? We call it mind because it is something separate from us. When we say "I think," notice the structure: "I" is the subject; "think" is the verb—the act of the mind. The thinker and the thought are not the same. And as strange as that may sound, sit with this: if you are not the mind, then what are you?

I learned this in the most brutal way imaginable—when I was drowning in suicidal ideation. Deep down, I didn't want to die. Something within me wanted to live. And yet, my mind was spinning with thoughts of death. Today, we even describe it accurately: "I have thoughts of suicide." Yes—you have them, but you are not them. Thoughts are not ownership; they are visitors.

These thoughts, like movie trailers, play in your head, over and over again. Some trailers are yours, drawn from lived experiences. Others are residuals—echoes passed down from generations. This is why therapists ask about family history, why doctors inquire about genetic conditions. What we call "hereditary mental health issues" is another way of saying ancestral inheritance—not just biologically, but energetically.

The point is simple, yet life-altering: you are not your mind, and you are not your thoughts. Think of the mind as ROM—read-only memory in a computer. Permanent storage. Thoughts, on the other hand, are RAM—temporary, fleeting processes running through the system. The mind processes emotional memories, and those emotional imprints create habits, behaviors, and conditioning. The mind is a motor powered by old fuel. And the performance of the car—your life—depends on what that fuel consists of.

This is why understanding the mind is not a luxury; it is survival on the highest level. Because until you understand the instrument that has been steering your ship, you will continue to mistake its voice for your own.

"Mind" Meditation

Close your eyes and ask yourself: *How can I be thinking and hearing myself at the same time? Who is hearing the thinking?* And when the thinking stops, what or who remains as the awareness in that silence? Something—while you are silent—is still there. It sees, it hears, it feels, it senses without effort. It is observing everything at once, without trying.

We often disregard silence because silence doesn't feel like anything. It seems empty, void, pointless. Yet in silence, the mind rests. In silence, the observer becomes the observed. In silence, the "I" in *I am happy* reveals itself. Notice this: "am" is the active mind. "Happy" is the state of personality or emotion. When silence arrives, "am" dissolves, and what remains is pure "I"—consciousness without the need for labels. "I" can now observe the "happy" like a floating cloud, from a distance… unattached, without Ego.

In this state, you witness thoughts and emotions without becoming them. You see them as passing clouds in the sky of awareness. Silence is not absence—it is a mirror. And in that mirror, you see the truth that was hidden beneath noise.

Often, when we are in conversation with someone, we don't really listen; we react from our programming, from experiences that shaped our perspectives, from beliefs we never questioned. Every word we speak is a projection of past conditioning. It isn't until we awaken that we realize we have been living as a byproduct of what has happened to us, both the good and the bad. By experience, I mean everything: birth, childhood, parenting, schooling, trauma, influence, religion, and even the name you were given. Every fragment of your identity is stitched together by memory.

Meditation tears open that fabric, not to destroy it, but to show you the thread. In meditation, the mind becomes an object of observation. Silence becomes the home of awareness. And awareness—that wordless knowing—reveals what the mind cannot comprehend.

When I experienced suicidal ideations, I also experienced fear—fear of dying, fear of losing control. But fear, I came to understand, was just an idea wearing the mask of truth. An idea that triggered emotion, and emotion that manifested in the body as feeling. Those feelings erupted as rapid heartbeats, shallow breath, trembling hands—what the world calls a panic attack.

As the panic escalated, my mind screamed for answers. And because I did not yet have the awareness or the language for what was happening, my suffering intensified. Thoughts felt real because my body was feeling them. And that is what I want you to understand: when thoughts create an emotional response, you begin to feel your thoughts—and in feeling them, you believe them.

The lesson I pulled from that abyss was simple but profound: I am not what I feel. I am not what I think. I am not the storm in my chest. And yet, I could only understand this truth by facing it—by allowing the panic to break me open.

Meditation became my lifeline. It gave me space between thought and action, between fear and choice. It allowed me to watch the waves instead of drowning in them. Little by little, meditation granted me agency. Each session, each breath, was a rebellion against the old self. The self that had been buried under decades of conditioning.

I began to see that the grave I feared was not physical death—it was the grave of my ego. And in that grave lay every identity I had clung to, every story I had called "me." To rise from that burial, the old had to die. Not violently, but inevitably.

And here's what I learned: the ego doesn't truly die—it steps aside. It learns its rightful place as a servant, not a master. And in that space, the higher self—the timeless witness—emerges, quiet and steady, like dawn breaking after a relentless night.

Emotion

So what are emotions? Why do we need them? What purpose do they serve? When we think of emotions, some come wrapped in light and others in shadow. Some we welcome; others we resist. The truth is, every emotion is an echo of what you are living now—a reciprocating effect of how you interpret life. Whether you stand in the brightness of joy or the storm of grief, your perspective bends reality through the lens of feeling.

Emotions are not a weakness. They are intelligence—raw and unfiltered, capable of shaping nations and toppling them, of building worlds and burning them to ash. With the right emotion, you can alter the course of history. And history remembers those who did. Emotions have been with us since before memory began. They are the invisible threads that connect us to people, places, and things. Without them, life would lose its weight, its texture, its meaning. Without them, you would be a silent machine wandering through a simulation—scrolling endlessly, waking and sleeping inside loops without depth or purpose. Emotions make life real. They make it yours.

An emotion is not just a reaction; it is the living bridge where the inner world meets the outer, where the unseen soul touches visible reality. It gives shape to your thoughts, color to your experiences, and substance to your relationships. It is what makes you care, what makes you act, what makes you fall to your knees in grief or rise in defiance. Emotions are not decoration—they are architecture. They build the reality you live in every day.

The ancients understood this better than we do now. Even the language tells the truth: the word emotion springs from the Latin *emovere*—to move out, to stir up. In Greek, its root is the same: energy in motion. Emotions are kinetic—they are not still; they seek expression. Picture a river. Left to flow, it nourishes the land. Dam it, and the water swells, crashes, and floods with destruction. So too with emotions. Repressed, they become storms. A tsunami in the nervous system. Unchecked, they wreck everything in their path. Honored, they become teachers—guiding, cleansing, transforming.

To work with emotions, you must first understand that they are not abstract—they are physics. They are motion. They carry force, and in physics, a force can change the speed, the direction, and even the shape of an object. Now apply that truth to yourself. Every emotion you feel shifts the trajectory of your life. It speeds you toward something or slows you down. It shapes your decisions, your habits, your reality. The body does not escape the law of energy. It is the canvas on which emotions paint themselves.

You can't think your way out of an emotional storm because the mind is the architect of its creation. It is like trying to put out a fire with more fire. The solution is not in the instrument that created the problem. Einstein knew this when he said you cannot solve a problem with the same level of thinking that created it. And yet, this is what most of us do—thinking harder, analyzing deeper, trying to reason with the roar inside us. We forget this simple truth: an emotion is not a thought. It is a physical event. It is energy in motion, moving through the nervous system like a current through a wire.

But here is the challenge: most people never question their emotions. They rarely ask: where did this come from? Why is it here? What is its root? Instead, we default to blame. We project the storm outward, hurling lightning at whoever or whatever stands closest. "Why is this happening to me?" becomes our mantra. Rarely do we pause and wonder: What is life trying to show me through this?

I was guilty of this, too. Before my awakening, I wanted answers. I wanted to locate emotions like coordinates on a map, as if their roots lived outside of me. I wanted to believe they were random, scientific, something beyond my control—so I could escape responsibility. But solitude stripped that illusion bare. The truth I found was inconvenient for my ego but liberating for my soul: emotions were not cosmic accidents. They were mirrors of my own perspectives. They were messages written in a language I had never learned to read.

And this revelation unraveled another thread: if my perspective shapes my emotional reality, then I am not my emotions. And if my perspective can change, then I am not my perspective either. So what am I? Who is the "I" that observes these shifting states? What is the force that witnesses joy, rage, grief, and does not drown in any of them? These questions pierced through the fog like arrows, leading me toward an intelligence deeper than thought—a consciousness capable of holding emotion without being defined by it.

Understand this: emotions are not enemies. They are signals. They are the body's way of saying, *Look here. Something needs attention.* They are not punishments. They are invitations. They rise when you are out of alignment, when your inner world is at war with your outer world. Ignore them, and they grow louder. Listen, and they lead you home.

Body – How Energies Are Released

When I began to understand my condition—not from books, but from the battlefield within me—my healing began, and the void I had feared for so long started to take shape. What once felt like an infinite abyss transformed into a tesseract of meaning, folding and unfolding layers I had never known existed. For the first time in my life, I could feel—not in fragments, not as flashes of sensation, but as a whole being. I began to understand, not through the intellect of the mind, but through the silent knowing of consciousness.

Crossing that threshold felt like stepping into another dimension—a realm where time slowed, not literally, but perceptually. I could sense people differently. Their words carried weight beyond language; their intentions revealed themselves like echoes in a canyon. And why? Because I finally understood myself. When you know your own shadows, you recognize them in others.

But this awakening was not soft. It tore me open in ways I wasn't prepared for. Strong suicidal ideations became the blade that pierced the fabric of space and time and forced me out of perception into perspective. In that rupture, I saw the mechanics of my suffering: I was not my thoughts. I was not my emotions. These, I realized, were simply energies in motion—streams of force moving through the nervous system, demanding release.

So I asked myself the question that changed everything: if I am not my emotions, and emotions are nothing but energy in motion, then what do I need to do with this energy? The answer was simple, though not easy: I needed to move it. Energy demands motion. If it cannot flow, it stagnates. If it stagnates, it poisons.

At the time, the only ways I knew to move energy were raw, primal, and unrefined: crying until my ribs ached, screaming until my throat burned, sometimes even vomiting without sickness because the body needed a purge. These were not graceful acts—they were survival acts. I learned this through research, yes, but more through self-experience. And let me say this plainly: you don't choose these releases; they choose you when the weight becomes unbearable.

Now, I know this may sound unsettling, even uncomfortable to read. But discomfort is the price of truth. These acts were not weaknesses—they were the first steps toward freedom. They were proof that what we call "emotions" are not abstract moods; they are physiological storms. They live in the body, they alter your breath, your pulse, your posture. And if you don't release them, they calcify into chronic tension, into illness, into patterns of self-destruction.

This is why I say, with absolute conviction, that the first stage of healing is physical. You cannot bypass the body and leap into enlightenment. You cannot intellectualize your way out of trauma. Feelings live in flesh, and flesh must release what it holds.

Everything I experienced—PTSD, depression, panic attacks—was somatic. My thoughts became feelings, and those feelings crystallized into sensations so vivid they felt like reality itself. That's why suicidal thoughts feel so real—because the body is feeling them. Can you imagine what it means to feel your thoughts? To watch a movie trailer in your head and experience every frame in your nervous system? That was my reality.

And this is why I emphasize this truth: you are not your thoughts, and you are not your emotions. But as long as they remain unprocessed, they will hijack your being and make you live as their servant. The key is to learn the art of transmutation—the conscious movement of energy through the body.

Here's the paradox: society romanticizes the idea of "feeling your emotions," but few understand what that really means. To feel is not to wallow endlessly in emotional loops. It is not to build a home in grief or rage. Feeling is a process—a tool, not a lifestyle. You enter it with awareness, you let the energy move, and then you let it go. Healing becomes toxic when it becomes identity.

I often compare this to systems. Every system has a purpose and an endpoint. If you keep reliving the same emotions without resolution, you are no longer healing—you are reinforcing the wound. That's why understanding different modalities of release is essential: breath-work, movement, sound, art, and even primal screaming when necessary. Because the body is not a prison—it is a portal.

And here is where I'll give you an analogy most people might not expect: healing is like playing Minecraft. In that game, you build the world you imagine, but to build, you first have to earn the tools. You choose the terrain, the materials, and the level of difficulty. You decide whether to survive or create. Life is no different. Every belief, every habit, every trauma is a block in your personal architecture. And if awakening happens in your forties or fifties, like it did for me, imagine the demolition required. You are not just rearranging furniture—you are dismantling a skyscraper built on decades of conditioning.

You've spent a lifetime stacking blocks of identity—shaped by religion, culture, politics, and pain—until your world looks solid and immovable. Then one day, awakening comes like a sledgehammer and says: Tear it down. Not all at once, not violently, but deliberately—block by block. Do you see the magnitude of that work? Do you see why healing feels like death? Because in a way, it is.

Here is the truth you cannot escape: the reality you call "life" is not as real as you think. It is a mirror—a projection of your inner architecture. Your external world is built from the vibrations of your internal state. And if that state is fractured, your life will reflect the fracture. That's why energy work matters. Because when you move the energy within, you rewrite the architecture of your existence.

Energy

Energy… I could write entire volumes about it, yet for the sake of this book, I will compress it into three pillars: energy, vibration, and frequency. We hear these words everywhere—"everything is energy," "raise your vibration," "shift your frequency"—and for a time, I too repeated them like mantras without ever questioning what they meant. They sounded powerful, mystical, and affirming. But what does it truly mean to raise your vibration or align your energy? What does it actually mean when people say "everything is energy"?

This is where I ask you to suspend disbelief—not because I want you to accept a spiritual cliché, but because I want you to ground yourself in what science already knows and what ancient wisdom has never forgotten. Let's begin here: modern physics defines energy as the capacity to do work. Energy exists in various forms: kinetic energy (energy in motion), potential energy (stored energy), thermal energy (heat), and electrical energy (current moving through matter). Energy can transform from one form to another, but it cannot be created or destroyed. This is the law of conservation—unbreakable, universal, eternal.

Why does this matter? Because it reveals something astonishing: the same law that governs the motion of planets governs the emotions in your body. The frustration sitting in your chest, the joy rising in your heart, the grief pressing against your throat—

these are not abstract feelings. They are energy. And energy follows laws.

When you are angry and don't express it, that energy does not vanish. It stores. It burrows into tissues. It coils like a spring in your nervous system, waiting for release. When you carry grief unspoken, it does not dissolve—it becomes weight, heavy in the lungs, slow in the breath. When you bury shame, it calcifies into posture: the rounded shoulders, the downward gaze, the voice that struggles to rise. This is why the body becomes a biography. Every gesture, every ache, every tension is a sentence in the story of energy.

Now, let's go deeper. If everything is energy, then every object you see, every breath you take, every thought you think is a transfer of force in motion. Every atom in your body is 99.9999999% empty space, but within that space, electrons spin in ceaseless motion. That spin is vibration. That vibration creates frequency. And that frequency defines reality as you know it.

Einstein said it best: $E = mc^2$. Energy and mass are two faces of the same coin. Matter is frozen energy, slowed to a state we can perceive as solid. You, me, this planet, the stars, the black holes at the edge of the cosmos—all of it is energy clothed in form. The Big Bang was not matter exploding—it was energy expanding, untamed and infinite, birthing the illusion of solidity.

So the next time you hear someone say "everything is energy," don't roll your eyes. Don't dismiss it as woo-woo. Understand it for what it truly is: the most profound truth science has ever confirmed. Energy is the root of all things. You are not separate from that truth. You are not a machine in a universe of dead matter—you are the universe vibrating in human form. And the more conscious you become of this, the more power you have—not the power to control life, but the power to harmonize with it.

Vibration

Vibration is not a mystical concept—it is the foundation of reality. Strip away the poetry, strip away the spiritual associations, and you arrive at pure physics: vibration is the rhythmic motion of particles.

Every atom in your body vibrates. Every cell hums with motion. Even what appears solid—your desk, your bones, a mountain—is vibrating at a microscopic level. This is not theory; it is observable.

Electrons orbit their nucleus in constant motion, generating energy fields. These fields interact, collide, and influence one another. Every object has a natural frequency—a resonant signature that determines how it responds to force. This is why engineers build bridges with harmonic frequencies in mind, why a singer can shatter glass with pitch alone. It's also why your body, with its billions of vibrating cells, is a living symphony.

Your organs each have a vibration. Your brain produces measurable waves—beta when focused, alpha when calm, theta when dreaming, and delta when in deep restorative sleep. Even your heart vibrates with such coherence that science now measures its electromagnetic field several feet beyond your body. Modern biophysics goes further, revealing that your cells emit photons—tiny bursts of light—proof that life radiates.

And here's the wonder: when two vibrations meet, they do not remain indifferent—they seek harmony. This is called entrainment. Pendulum clocks in the same room eventually swing in sync. A tuning fork strikes, and a nearby string hums in resonance. Humans are no different. We attune to the energy around us—sometimes without knowing. That is why a calm presence can soothe chaos, and why anxiety spreads like fire in a crowded room. Vibration is not a metaphor—it is mechanics.

Temperature? It's vibration. Heat is the speed of molecular motion. Sound? Vibration rippling through the air. Light? Vibration in the electromagnetic field. Even color is frequency translated by perception. When you understand this, you stop seeing vibration as a mystical tagline and start seeing it as the pulse of existence.

Pythagoras spoke of the "music of the spheres," believing the cosmos moved like a grand symphony. Today, quantum physicists echo this truth through string theory: the smallest building blocks of the universe are not particles, but vibrating strings of energy. From the first sound that shattered silence to the hum of your heartbeat, creation has always been vibration.

Frequency

If vibration is motion, then frequency is the measure of that motion—the rate at which energy oscillates in a given time frame. Frequency is the rhythm quantified. It is counted in Hertz: cycles per second. A string vibrating 440 times a second gives us the musical note A, but this principle extends far beyond sound.

Your brain operates on frequencies. Beta waves dominate when you're alert and solving problems. Alpha emerges when you're calm, reflective. Theta appears in deep meditation and REM sleep. Delta hums when you sink into the deepest rest. These are not abstract states—they are measurable realities. Your consciousness tunes itself like an instrument, moment by moment.

Your heart, too, radiates frequency. Its electromagnetic field synchronizes with your nervous system and, astonishingly, influences those around you. Studies from the HeartMath Institute show that when people achieve emotional coherence—states of gratitude, compassion—their heart rhythm stabilizes, and this harmony extends to others nearby. Entrainment at work again.

And then there is Earth itself. Our planet vibrates at a baseline frequency of about 7.83 Hz—the Schumann Resonance. Ancient mystics called this the rhythm of life, and now science agrees: it's the heartbeat of the Earth. What's more, this frequency mirrors the alpha-theta border in the human brain—the state of deep calm and creativity. Coincidence? Or a reminder that we were never meant to live out of sync with nature?

The electromagnetic spectrum tells the same story. Light, radio waves, X-rays—all are frequencies at different scales. What we call visible light is just a tiny sliver. Infrared hums below it. Ultraviolet vibrates above it. Beyond that, waves continue endlessly, unseen yet real. The fact that we can't perceive them doesn't negate their existence. Our senses are filters, not measures of reality.

So what does this mean for your life? Everything. Because your state of being—your clarity, your chaos, your peace, your despair—resonates at a frequency. And like a radio, if you don't like the station, you have to tune. Not by wishing, but by conscious alignment. By becoming aware of what you frequently do, because your frequency is built on your patterns. The thoughts you repeat. The emotions you indulge. The environments you marinate in.

And here is where the spiritual truth and the scientific fact shake hands: raising your vibration, shifting your frequency—it isn't magic. It's mechanics. You don't need crystals or chants, though both can serve as tools. What you need is presence. Breath. Stillness. Movement. Coherence between heart and mind. You need to understand that the body is an antenna, and your choices are the dial.

The Ancients

Now we stand at the threshold where science and mysticism touch—the place where the language of numbers begins to sound like the language of spirit.

Because long before we spoke of electrons and quarks, the ancients were already whispering truths we now confirm in laboratories: all is vibration, all is energy, all is one.

The Hermetic texts of Egypt declared, *Nothing rests; everything moves; everything vibrates.* In India, the sages spoke of *Nada Brahma*—the world is sound—not metaphorical sound, but the original resonance from which creation unfolded. In China, Qi was not an abstract concept; it was a life force, moving through meridians like rivers through a landscape. The Greeks sang of the "music of the spheres," believing the cosmos moved in harmonic proportion.

What were they pointing to? The same reality our quantum scientists now describe in different words: a universe woven from oscillations, a fabric of frequency. The ancients did not need microscopes to know this—they felt it. They attuned their bodies and minds to these rhythms through breath, chant, ritual, and stillness. They did not separate science from spirit; to them, knowing the world and knowing the self were one and the same act.

Look closer. In the Vedic tradition, sound syllables—mantras—were not mere symbols but carriers of vibration designed to harmonize the individual with the cosmos. In the Hebrew scriptures, creation began with a spoken word: *Let there be light.* The Word—the vibration—preceded the form. Indigenous shamans drummed not for entertainment but for alignment, knowing that rhythm reorganizes the nervous system, calling it back to coherence. Every chant, every ritual was a recalibration, not a performance.

The ancients didn't say "raise your vibration" as a trend—they lived it as a practice. They fasted to lighten the body's density. They breathed to clear the channels of energy. They danced to restore flow. They sat in silence to hear the hum beneath existence. And now, science measures what they knew intuitively: meditation shifts brain waves, breath alters heart coherence, sound reorganizes neural patterns. What the ancients embodied, we now plot on charts.

The irony is sharp: in a world drowning in data, we have lost the wisdom to feel. We talk about energy like a commodity, as if alignment were an app we could download. But alignment is not instant—it is intimacy with life itself. And the ancients knew this. They knew that the language of the universe is not spoken in words but in resonance. They knew that when you tune yourself to that language, you stop fighting life and start flowing with it.

So when I tell you that energy, vibration, and frequency matter, I am not asking you to believe a spiritual slogan; I am inviting you to remember what every culture, every tradition, every mystic has been trying to tell us for thousands of years: you are not separate from the cosmos. You are its echo, its instrument, its song.

The Fragmented Self

If everything is energy, if every cell hums with frequency, then why do so many of us feel so broken? Why do we live fractured, anxious, perpetually restless? This is not just a philosophical puzzle—it is an existential wound.

The answer is rhythm. Or rather, the loss of it. We were designed to move with the cadence of nature:

light and dark, inhale and exhale, effort and surrender. Our nervous system was built for coherence—a state where heart, breath, and brain harmonize like instruments in a single song. But modern life is a dissonant symphony. We wake to alarms instead of sunrises. We eat in haste, speak in fragments, scroll endlessly through waves of artificial stimulus. Our bodies remain in fight-or-flight long after the danger is gone, because the danger is never gone—it hums in the background as constant noise.

We call it anxiety. We call it burnout. We call it depression. But beneath the labels, the truth is simple: we are out of tune. Our internal systems no longer entrain with the earth that birthed them. The signal is broken. And when coherence collapses, identity fractures. You feel the split every time you say yes when your soul screams no, every time you perform instead of living, every time you trade stillness for speed.

I know this fracture intimately. It nearly killed me. If you have read the beginning of this book, you know my nights of panic, the ideations that clawed at my sanity, the ER visits that left me hollow. What I didn't understand then—but do now—is that I was not just emotionally shattered. I was energetically incoherent. My field was noise, static, interference. And the body, loyal to its nature, responded with alarms: pounding heart, shallow breath, a brain looping in terror. Not because I was weak, but because I was out of rhythm with myself.

Here is the paradox: this disconnection, as devastating as it feels, is also the invitation. Because only when the instrument is out of tune can you hear the need to tune it. Only when the pieces scatter can you begin the sacred work of recollection. And this is the work of healing—not to become something new, but to return to coherence, to restore the song you were born to sing.

The ancients called this alignment. Modern science calls it homeostasis. I call it remembering, and I also call it transformation. Because the truth is, you have never lost what you are—you have only forgotten how to feel it. And when you remember, when you silence the noise and listen for the hum beneath the chaos, you will find that what was fragmented was never broken.

It was waiting. Waiting to be heard, to be felt, to be lived. It was pain awaiting transformation. Healing.

Because what scatters will always seek to return.

Chapter Five
Trauma

> **"Out of chaos, stars are born."**
>
> — *Charles Chaplin*

If you ask the textbooks, they'll tell you trauma is a response to a deeply distressing or disturbing event that overwhelms a person's ability to cope. They'll talk about fight, flight, or freeze. They'll use words like dysregulation and hypervigilance. And while that's not wrong, it's barely scratching the surface of what trauma truly is and what it does to the human experience. Because trauma is not just the story of what happened—it's the residue of what couldn't be processed, the energy that was never discharged, the breath that never came. It doesn't live in the past tense of an event—it lives in the present tense of your body, in the nervous system that learned to adapt by shutting down or staying on high alert, in the way your awareness narrows when something feels familiar but you can't explain why.

Trauma is not the knife—it's the wound. And the wound can exist without a blade, without a visible scar, without any evidence at all except for the way your chest tightens when someone raises their voice, or the way you go numb in the middle of a conversation because your body remembers something your mind has buried so deep it feels like it never happened. Trauma isn't always loud. Sometimes it's quiet. Sometimes it whispers through silence, through the absence of what you needed most. Sometimes it begins in neglect, in abandonment, in a love that was inconsistent or a presence that was withdrawn. It can begin not with a scream, but with an empty room.

Science now confirms what mystics have whispered for centuries: trauma lives not only in the mind, but in the body, and deeper still, in the energy that sustains us. It imprints itself on the nervous system, shapes neural pathways, and changes how the vagus nerve responds to safety or threat. Trauma teaches the body to survive the past in the present.

Even when the danger is gone, the body behaves as if it's still there. The heart races without a lion in the room. Muscles tense without a blow being thrown, and the breath shortens without a single hand raised against you. Because to the body, memory is not in words—it's in sensation. And when sensation becomes overwhelming, the mind disconnects. That's dissociation, and it's why you can't "think" your way out of trauma. Because trauma is not a thought, it's a frequency. It's a rhythm your body learned to play when life demanded survival over peace.

For years, I thought trauma was something that happened to other people—victims of crimes, survivors of disasters, or Veterans. I never saw it in myself, even though I served eight years in the Army and wore it like armor I couldn't take off. I deployed to Afghanistan twice and to Iraq, and traveled and trained across the country in different environments and with foreign militaries. I saw things that can't be unseen in war and during training. I heard sounds that still echo in my bones, like half-blown-up mountains from the amount of enemy weapons and explosive caches found in Afghanistan. Incoming and outgoing mortar rounds every seven days when the moon was at its brightest, and I was in a deep sleep in Iraq. IED explosions detonated by the lead vehicle—the flash traveled faster than the sound of the boom. Radio calls rushing medics, situational reports of wounded friends. Gun trucks struck by RPK fire, RPGs missing my vehicle, the turret gunner shouting for more .50 caliber rounds, or the news of fallen soldiers.

At some point, I stopped giving a fuck. What once seemed like chaos became the new normal. You learn to roll over on your cot at 0200 hours instead of seeking shelter at the sound of mortar rounds—just to get some sleep. At some point, you desensitize. Explosions become a new genre. Gunfire and tracer rounds feel like fireworks, helicopter rides become bassinets, and moments of calm and silence are found during QRF (Quick Reaction Force)— while awaiting to be activated. Teenagers turn into warriors before becoming adults.

Military Service

One month after high school (July, 2001)

Afghanistan, 2003

Afghanistan, 2003

FOB Kalsu, Iraq (2004)

And so I did what most soldiers do: I kept it together like everyone else. I didn't talk about it. I stayed strong. Because strength was survival, and survival was the only option. But when I came home, the battlefield came with me. It followed me into my sleep, into my relationships, into every quiet moment I tried to have. I thought I was fine—until I wasn't. Until my body collapsed under the weight of everything I never allowed myself to feel.

I became my kids' drill instructor—and a pain in the ass. Everything was about control and being ready for the unexpected. Honestly, this is the part I hated most about myself: how I raised my voice at my little girls and demanded perfection in how I was raising them. I remember my ex-wife telling me to leave the table while we were eating because I kept correcting my kids. It was an unpleasant experience for the family. I didn't see it at the time, but I was certainly hurting my family with my personal trauma. That night was the first time my ex-wife checked me, and I knew there was something wrong with me.

I got up from the table, walked straight out the door, and started walking without knowing where I was going. Then I began jogging and ended up at a nearby park. The sun had set. I hid in the dark and began to sob, pounding the earth with my fists. I was tired of myself. The struggle was real. My life felt like it amounted to nothing—even though I had it all. I screamed, "I just want this to stop, please." Eventually, I collected myself and began walking home.

The VA (Department of Veterans Affairs) called it PTSD—Post-Traumatic Stress Disorder. Later, they added TBI—Traumatic Brain Injury. Anxiety. Depression. A cocktail of labels and medications meant to manage the aftermath of too much chaos compressed into too little time. And yet, none of those diagnoses told the whole truth. Because the truth is, my trauma didn't just start with war. It started long before that. It started in childhood, in the silence I mistook for safety, in the distance I interpreted as rejection, in the moments when love felt conditional and presence felt rare. It started with a nervous system that learned to self-parent before it even knew what the word meant.

And maybe that's what trauma really is: the moment the body says, "I can't hold this anymore." It's not weakness—it's biology. It's the system becoming so overwhelmed that it can no longer integrate what's happening, so it stores it instead. It locks it down in fascia, in muscle fibers, in the rhythm of your breath, in the way your eyes scan every room for danger, even when you're safe at home. Stored energy becomes stagnant energy. Stagnant energy becomes a field—a vibration—that colors everything you do. It's why chaos keeps finding its way back, even when you swear you've closed the door. It's why you end up in the same relationships, the same arguments, the same cycles you promised yourself you'd break because your frequency doesn't lie. And if trauma taught your body that love feels like pain or safety feels like absence, you will unconsciously seek the familiar—even when it hurts.

This is why we can't talk about trauma without talking about energy. Trauma contracts the field. It distorts your coherence. The heart and brain, which are designed to work in harmony, fall out of rhythm. Your electromagnetic field shrinks, your resonance drops, and you start living in survival states instead of creation states. This isn't woo-woo—it's measurable. HeartMath Institute has shown us how coherence affects everything from emotional regulation to immunity. When you're in survival mode, your heart rate variability plummets. Your breath becomes shallow. Your mind loops. You lose access to the prefrontal cortex—the part of you that can plan, create, and imagine. You're stuck in the limbic system, hijacked by fear. And fear has a frequency. It hums low and heavy, pulling everything in your life into that same dense vibration.

So when we say trauma is not just emotional, what we really mean is that trauma is multidimensional. It is physical, psychological, neurological, and energetic. It's in your cells, your circuits, your stories. It's in your epigenetics—the way your ancestors' survival strategies get coded into your DNA. Studies now show that trauma can be passed down for three, even four generations. That means the anxiety you feel when someone raises their voice might not even belong to you. It might belong to your grandmother, who grew up in a war zone, or your father, who learned to fear silence because silence meant someone wasn't coming home. And this isn't an excuse—it's an explanation. One that frees you from shame and invites you into responsibility. Because if it didn't start with you, maybe it can end with you.

But here's the part no one told me: trauma isn't your identity. It's not a life sentence. It's a signal. It's your body saying, "Come back. Come back to awareness. Come back to rhythm. Come back to yourself." Healing doesn't begin in the mind—it begins in the moment you stop running from the body. It begins when you stop saying "I'm fine" and start asking, "What am I feeling?" It begins when you notice the way your shoulders never drop, the way your jaw is always tight, the way your breath feels like a ration instead of a river. It begins when you name it—not to relive it, but to release it. Because the body is not your enemy, it's your compass. And when you learn to listen, it will lead you back to a coherence that feels like home.

And that's why this chapter exists. Not to give you more definitions, but to give you permission. Permission to feel. Permission to question the narratives you inherited. Permission to stop pretending that being strong means being silent. Because strength is not the absence of pain—it's the willingness to face it. To hold it and to breathe through it until it loosens its grip. To choose presence over performance and remember that you are not the wound—you are the one who has the power to heal it. To transform it.

Neglect – The Silent Wound

If trauma is the wound of disconnection, then neglect is the trauma of absence, and what makes it so dangerous is that it rarely announces itself with drama. There are no headlines for neglect, no broken glass, no shattered screams, because neglect hides in the quiet. It lingers in empty spaces where love should have been and wasn't. It sits in the gaps between presence and attention, like a silent architect shaping how we see ourselves, others, and the entire world around us.

Clinically, neglect is the failure to meet a person's basic physical, emotional, or psychological needs—needs that are not luxuries but lifelines, especially in childhood when attachment is oxygen and safety is everything. Safety. Comfort. Touch. Validation. Presence. When these are missing, the nervous system reorganizes itself around the void. It hardens where it should soften. It braces where it should breathe. It learns survival instead of trust, self-reliance instead of connection. And in that adjustment, something sacred gets lost.

But here's the part that cuts the deepest: neglect doesn't always come from malice. More often than not, it blooms in the soil of survival. The parents who neglected you may have been drowning themselves, carrying the weight of their own unspoken wounds. They didn't wake up thinking, *I will ignore my child today*. No—most believed they were doing the best they could. And maybe they were.

I know this firsthand.

When I was seven years old, I stepped into a new world—America—a land that promised everything but offered nothing for free. We left Guatemala chasing opportunity, but opportunity came at a cost: my parents' presence. My father worked three jobs, his hands always moving, his eyes rarely still long enough to meet mine. My mother spent nights caring for other people's children so she could bring money home to feed her own.

I can see their love now. I can honor their sacrifice. But the little boy I was didn't understand love in the language of absence. He only understood distance. He only knew what it felt like to need and not receive. And so, like every child, I turned the emptiness into a story—a story that said, *Maybe I'm not enough to stay for. Maybe I have to earn love. Maybe if I work harder, prove more, become more… they won't leave me behind.*

That story didn't stay in childhood. It grew roots in my nervous system and became the soil from which every relationship, every choice, every identity would sprout. And this is what most people never realize: neglect is not just emotional—it's neurological. It shapes the wiring of your brain, the tone of your vagus nerve, and the rhythm of your breath. It trains your amygdala to anticipate loss. It teaches your body to live in a low hum of hypervigilance, scanning for threats that never come and bracing for absence even when you're surrounded by love.

And it's not just in the brain—it's in the field. Neglect carries a vibration. It contracts your energy, shrinks your presence, makes your frequency tentative, cautious, unsure. When love was inconsistent or care was conditional, your entire being learns to broadcast a signal that says, *I'll stay small so I don't get hurt. I'll do more so you'll stay.* And that signal shapes everything—who you attract, how you speak, what you tolerate.

And unless someone names it, the cycle repeats. Fathers who grew up unseen become fathers who are always busy. Mothers who learned to silence themselves raise daughters who swallow their truth. Entire bloodlines humming with the frequency of neglect because no one paused long enough to hear the silence screaming beneath the surface.

This is why neglect is the silent wound. It doesn't bleed. It echoes.

Lives Built Around It

Not everyone who grows up neglected spirals into chaos. Some build kingdoms. Some turn the absence into ambition, the void into velocity. They become the achievers, the providers, the fixers, the ones who hold everyone else together while quietly falling apart inside. They become the leaders, the first responders, the soldiers, the CEOs, the counselors—the people others lean on without realizing what it costs to be that strong.

And on the surface, it looks admirable. Noble. A triumph of willpower. But under the surface, something else is true: much of that success is survival in disguise.

Neglect doesn't always create dysfunction. Sometimes it creates over-functioning. When your needs weren't met, you learn to meet everyone else's. When no one came for you, you became the one who always shows up. When you were invisible, you vowed to be seen—even if it meant burning yourself alive to light up someone else's world.

It sounds heroic, and in many ways, it is. But heroism rooted in neglect is a fragile empire. Because the same nervous system that once learned to numb in order to cope now depends on busyness to feel safe. The same energy field that once contracted around fear now expands only when validated by achievement. And what looks like freedom—financial success, social status, the house, the car, the respect—is often just a beautifully decorated cage built out of the same belief that started in childhood: *I have to do more to be enough.*

And here's the tragedy: the world rewards that belief. It celebrates the grind. It glorifies the hustle. It crowns the overachiever without asking what ghost they're running from. And so the cycle hides in plain sight. Generational. Cultural. Invisible but everywhere.

This is what people don't understand: trauma doesn't just create pain. It creates patterns. And one of the most seductive patterns born from neglect is performance. We perform for love. We perform for safety. We perform so much that we forget who we are when the curtain closes.

But here's the truth: no one teaches us: survival isn't living. And success that costs you yourself is just another form of abandonment.

My Story, Revisited

For most of my life, I thought I was doing everything right. I worked hard. I provided. I stayed busy. I wore strength like armor and silence like skin. And every time I said, *"I'm doing this for my family,"* I believed it. Every sacrifice. Every sleepless night. Every mile I ran to outrun the shadow of scarcity chasing me since childhood.

On paper, I was the success story—a soldier turned provider, a man who could endure anything. People looked at me and saw resilience. They saw control. But what they didn't see—what I didn't see—was the fracture beneath it all.

That fracture began when I was seven, standing in a country that didn't speak my language, watching my parents disappear into the grind that promised us a better life. My father is working three jobs, his hands calloused, his body exhausted, his presence absent. My mother spent nights with other people's children so she could feed her own. And I love them for that. I honor their sacrifice. But the child I was didn't understand love in the language of absence. He only knew the hollow feeling of being unseen.

And so I built a story. I told myself, *if I want love, I have to earn it. If I want to matter, I have to work for it.* And that story became the rhythm of my life—a low, constant vibration that hummed beneath every choice I made.

Years later, when I became a father, I repeated the pattern without even realizing it. I worked endlessly. I justified every absence with the same mantra: *I'm doing this for them.* And I believed it—just like my father had. Two men from different generations, living the same script, passing down the same frequency of absence, thinking it was love.

But survival has a breaking point. And mine came in the form of panic attacks so violent I thought I was dying. Out of nowhere, my chest locked up, my breath disappeared, my vision blurred, my arms went numb. And in that moment, I thought: *This is it. This is how it ends.*

I ended up in the ER three times in one week. They ran every test—heart, lungs, brain—and came back with the same answer: *You're fine.* But I wasn't fine. My body was screaming what my mouth never said: *I can't keep carrying this.* My nervous system was collapsing under decades of stored stress, suppressed emotion, and silence disguised as strength.

Those months broke me open. Six months of living inside a storm of fear and exhaustion, of waking up in the night gasping for air, of watching "movie trailers" of death play in my mind on loop, so vivid I believed them. If you've ever lived that, you know how real it feels. The body doesn't know the difference between memory and reality—it just responds. And mine responded like I was under attack 24/7.

But here's the paradox: that breakdown was the beginning of my becoming. Because when survival stops working, you have no choice but to feel. No choice but to see the cost of all the ways you've abandoned yourself. And that's when healing begins—not in fixing, not in doing, but in softening. In remembering. In coming home to what you left behind.

I realized something that changed everything: I had built an identity on a vibration of fear—a low hum that said, *Stay busy, stay strong, stay ahead, or you'll lose everything.* And when that vibration cracked, what spilled out wasn't weakness—it was truth. The truth that I had spent my life performing for love, I already had the right to feel. The truth was that I had been living as a soldier long after the war ended.

I share this because I know someone reading this is carrying the same weight, telling themselves the same lie: *I'm doing this for them.* But have you ever stopped long enough to ask: *What if all this doing is just a disguise? What if the life I've built is a monument to a wound I've never touched?*

Neglect doesn't just teach us how to endure—it teaches us how to avoid. How to stay busy enough not to feel. How to run so far from ourselves that collapse becomes the only way the body can call us back. But collapse is not the enemy. Collapse is the invitation.

And here's what I know now: healing begins when you stop. When you sit in the stillness you've spent decades outrunning, when you breathe through the fear instead of numbing it, when you choose presence over performance, awareness over autopilot, truth over the mask of strength.

I'm still learning this. Still undoing the architecture neglect built in me. Still softening the walls, I thought it would keep me safe. But if my story gives you anything, let it give you permission—permission to question the grind, the mask, the mission. Permission to ask not *"What am I doing all this for?"* but *"Who am I becoming while I do it?"*

Because once you trace the story back to its origin, you'll see what I saw: it didn't start with you. But it can end with you.

Abandonment

If neglect is the absence of care, abandonment is the absence of presence—not just what was never given, but what was once there and then lost, leaving behind a silence that doesn't fade. It's a rupture that creates more than emptiness—it creates an ache that burrows deep, shaping the nervous system and distorting the sense of safety for years, sometimes for life, unless awareness interrupts the pattern.

Clinically, abandonment is often defined as the withdrawal of emotional, physical, or psychological support at a time when connection is non-negotiable. And while the definition is accurate, it lacks the weight of the lived experience, because abandonment is not a concept—it's a wound. It's a wound that hums in the body long after the moment has passed, a vibration that colors how we love, how we trust, how we move through every relationship we build.

And the hardest part is that abandonment doesn't always look like someone slamming a door and walking away. Sometimes it hides in the subtleties—in a mother who is physically present but emotionally frozen, in a father who works endlessly to provide but forgets to look his child in the eye, in a partner who shares a bed but withholds their heart. It can happen without goodbyes, without threats, without obvious drama. And maybe that's why it's so hard to name—because when the wound is invisible, we convince ourselves it's not real.

But the body knows. The nervous system knows. When the presence that once felt like home disappears—whether suddenly or slowly—the body registers that loss as danger. And in childhood, that danger is catastrophic, because attachment isn't optional. It's survival. And when survival feels threatened, the body does what it must: it adapts.

Attachment science tells us what we see every day in human behavior: abandonment fractures trust at its root. The child learns not only that people leave, but that love can vanish without warning. The result? For some, hypervigilance means clinging tighter, crying louder, doing whatever it takes to keep them from leaving. Emotional shutdown in others—don't need, don't feel, don't expect, because needing hurts too much. These aren't choices; they're strategies. They're the nervous system's way of staying alive when connection feels like a gamble.

And here's the truth most never consider: these strategies don't dissolve with age. They travel. They hitch a ride into adulthood and show up in the ways we love and live. The person who checks their phone a hundred times, terrified of being ghosted, is not needy—they're carrying the echo of a wound. The person who pulls away every time things get deep isn't cold—they're bracing for a loss they've rehearsed since childhood.

And it's not just psychological—it's physiological. Chronic abandonment stress reshapes the brain. It floods the body with cortisol. It keeps the amygdala on high alert and the vagus nerve signaling threat even in safe spaces. And this state of constant survival isn't just a feeling—it's a frequency. You can feel it in the breath that never drops low, in the shoulders that never fully relax, in the eyes that scan the room even when there's nothing to fear.

And because energy attracts energy, that frequency becomes a magnet for more of the same. The child who grew up fearing loss often finds partners who are emotionally unavailable, inconsistent, unpredictable—not because they want pain, but because pain feels familiar, and familiarity feels safe even when it isn't. And so the cycle repeats—generation after generation, a silent thread woven through family systems, unspoken yet undeniable.

I've seen this in my own life. After the military, after years of wearing armor and calling it strength, I came home carrying more than physical scars—I carried patterns I didn't even know existed. Patterns of self-abandonment I had rehearsed since I was seven years old, when I stepped into a foreign land and watched my parents disappear into survival. They didn't mean to abandon me, but their absence—justified as it was—left a mark. And like most children, I didn't process it. I internalized it. I made it mean something about me: *I'm not enough to stay for. If I want love, I have to earn it.*

And so I spent decades earning. Hustling. Overperforming. I became selfish. Buying shit I did not need. Overspending. Becoming the man everyone could depend on and trying to convince myself I was worth something, while leaving myself behind in the process. Because abandonment doesn't just happen to us—it happens through us when we learn to leave ourselves in order to keep others close. We shrink so we don't scare them away. We silence our internal needs so we don't seem like a burden. We become whoever we need to be so no one else leaves—even if it means leaving our own soul behind.

But here's the paradox: it works at least for a while. People stay. They applaud our strength, our sacrifice, our loyalty. But the cost is enormous. Because every time you abandon yourself to keep someone else, you confirm the lie that started the cycle: *Who I am is not enough.*

Abandonment shows up in so many places we don't expect. In the daughter who grows up watching her father walk out the door for the last time, never realizing that moment will shape her sense of worth in every relationship she enters. In the boy whose mother leaves after years of fighting with his dad, teaching him that love is conditional, fragile, and temporary. These wounds don't disappear with time—they hide inside choices, inside patterns, inside the quiet places we avoid.

But the most dangerous kind of abandonment isn't when they leave—it's when we leave ourselves, when we ignore what we feel because we're afraid that feeling will cost us love. When we disconnect from our own bodies because being present means remembering the pain. When we live our entire lives performing for approval while starving for authenticity, that is self-abandonment—and it is the deepest betrayal of all.

And like every form of trauma, abandonment doesn't just alter behavior—it alters energy. It contracts your field. It creates a vibration of fear so subtle you might not notice it, but the world does. It hums through your posture, your tone, your choices. It draws people who resonate with it—not because the universe is cruel, but because energy seeks coherence, even when that coherence keeps us bound to our pain.

But here's the hope: what is patterned can be rewritten. What is wired can be rewired. What vibrates low can rise. And it begins not when someone else promises to stay, but when you promise yourself: *I will no longer leave me.*

Healing starts in the smallest moments—the pause before you overgive, the breath you take when the urge to chase rises, the softness you offer yourself when fear says, *They'll leave if you don't perform.* Healing begins when you sit in the stillness you've spent years avoiding and whisper to the child inside you, *I'm here now. I'm not going anywhere.*

Because when you stop abandoning yourself, the frequency shifts. Your energy expands. Your body exhales. And for the first time, you stop vibrating at the frequency of loss and start resonating with presence. Not because the world changed, but because you did.

You become the anchor you were searching for. You become the safe space your younger self never had. And from that place, love is no longer a gamble—it's a gift.

Abuse

Abuse is a word that carries weight, a word that makes people flinch, because it conjures images of bruises, screams, police reports, broken homes. But the truth is that abuse is not limited to what can be seen. It's not just what leaves marks on the body—it's what leaves imprints on the nervous system. It's what fractures the sense of safety in a way that lingers for decades, even in silence, even in the absence of physical evidence.

Clinically, abuse is described as the intentional or negligent mistreatment of another human being, resulting in harm—physical, emotional, psychological, or sexual. But definitions like that sanitize the lived experience. They reduce it to something measurable when, in reality, abuse is a distortion of love so profound it rewrites a person's entire sense of self. Abuse doesn't just hurt—it conditions. It conditions us to believe that love equals pain, that safety is unpredictable, that our worth is conditional, fragile, and subject to the moods or power of someone else.

And the most dangerous part? Abuse doesn't stay contained in one lifetime. It echoes through generations, passed down not because people are evil, but because people are wounded. If your father grew up in a home where fists spoke louder than words, where dominance was disguised as discipline, then his nervous system learned that control equals security. If your mother was raised on criticism instead of compassion, she may believe that harshness is care, that yelling is love, that shaming a child is a way to make them strong. These patterns don't disappear because someone says, *I'll never be like them.* They live in the body, in the vibration, in the subconscious programs we don't even know we're running.

This is why entire family trees can hum with the same low frequency of pain. Addiction is passed down like an heirloom. Violence is normalized as "just how it is." Silence carries the weight of unspoken trauma. And until someone stops long enough to name it, the cycle repeats—not because we choose it consciously, but because the body repeats what feels familiar, even when familiar is killing us.

And that is the truth no one wants to face: most people who abuse others were once abused themselves. The child who was hit learns that power comes through force. The child who was humiliated learns that control is survival. The child who was ignored learns to scream through rage because silence once felt like death. And so the wound becomes the weapon. The victim becomes the perpetrator, not out of malice, but out of unconscious repetition.

Abuse is not just physical. It's not just sexual. It's emotional. It's mental. It's in the tone of voice that breaks a child's spirit. It's in the manipulation disguised as love. It's in the gaslighting that makes someone question their own reality until they can no longer trust themselves. And each form of abuse does something devastating to the human spirit: it splits us from our own truth. It makes us doubt our worth. It teaches us to silence what hurts until the silence becomes a prison we can't escape.

But here's what most don't realize: abuse doesn't just live in memory—it lives in energy. It alters the vibration of the body. It contracts the field. It creates a resonance of fear, shame, and survival that becomes the baseline frequency of a life. This is why healing abuse isn't just about forgiving or forgetting. It's about recalibrating the entire system—mind, body, and field—back to coherence. Because until that happens, the patterns will repeat in some form, whether through chaos, control, addiction, or avoidance.

Physical Abuse

Physical abuse is the most visible, and yet even when it's visible, people look away. They turn their heads. They say, *It's not my business.* And when it's hidden—under sweaters in summer, behind closed doors, inside families that pride themselves on keeping secrets—it becomes a wound that grows roots in silence.

Physical abuse teaches the body something it was never meant to learn: that touch is dangerous, that love can hurt, that safety can turn into violence without warning. And the body remembers. Long after the bruises fade, the nervous system stays in fight-or-flight, bracing for impact that may never come but feels inevitable. The shoulders hunch without thinking. The breath shortens even in calm rooms. The jaw clenches at the sound of footsteps, because once, those footsteps meant pain.

Let me tell you about a little girl.

She was an infant when her mother left her father, too young to understand what was happening, too young to protest. She wouldn't meet her biological father until her teenage years. In his absence, her mother remarried. A new man stepped into the house, but not into her heart. Instead of love, he gave her fear. Instead of protection, he gave her bruises. And when she finally found the courage to run, to go to the police—the very system we teach children to trust—they sent her back home. Back to the fists. Back to the silence. Back to a mother who, for her own reasons, didn't protect her.

That kind of betrayal doesn't just hurt—it breaks something fundamental. And what breaks isn't just trust in others—it's trust in yourself. Because if the people who were supposed to keep you safe didn't, then safety becomes an illusion. And when safety feels like an illusion, the entire nervous system reorganizes around survival. That little girl learned to wear armor—an armor that looked like perfection, like strength, like control. But beneath the armor, the vibration of fear hummed so loud it shaped everything—how she loved, how she trusted, how she responded to every conflict for the rest of her life.

This is physical abuse. It doesn't end in childhood. It follows you into adulthood, into relationships, into parenting, into every moment where closeness feels like a trap. It shows up in the flinch when someone raises their hand, even in play. It shows up in the urge to control everything, because chaos once meant pain. It shows up in anger that erupts without warning, because anger feels safer than vulnerability.

And here's the generational link: if that girl never heals, if that vibration never shifts, the pain becomes a pattern. It becomes the tone in her voice when she disciplines her children. It becomes the energy in her home when stress rises. It becomes the subconscious belief passed down like a curse: *Love must hurt. Control is safety. Fear is normal.* And unless someone interrupts the cycle, the bruises may disappear, but the imprint never does.

Sexual Abuse

Sexual abuse is one of the most complex and misunderstood forms of trauma, largely because we've been conditioned to define it in narrow terms—violent assault, clear boundaries crossed. But the truth is, sexual abuse exists on a spectrum, and many who carry its scars were never "touched" in the way society imagines. Exposure, coercion, grooming, manipulation — these are also violations, and their impact can be just as profound as physical force.

I know this because I've lived it.

When I was four or five years old, I witnessed a teenager masturbate in front of me. He sat me on his lap and made me watch him. There was no physical contact, but that doesn't mean it wasn't abuse. That moment imprinted something in me—a confusion, a distortion of innocence, an energetic violation that I didn't even understand until decades later. And this is what people don't realize: abuse is not just about the body—it's about the nervous system. It's about the imprint of threat, the invasion of safety, the collapse of boundaries so early that you don't even know where "safe" ends and "danger" begins.

Sexual trauma doesn't always scream. Sometimes it whispers. It whispers shame into a child's sense of self. It whispers confusion into the way a teenager sees intimacy. It whispers distortion into an adult's relationships, teaching them to equate love with secrecy, desire with danger, pleasure with guilt. And because no one talks about it, the shame festers. The nervous system carries the freeze response like a secret, locking down the body every time vulnerability approaches.

And here's where energy comes in: sexual abuse doesn't just live in memory—it lives in frequency. It leaves a residue in the field. It drops the vibration of innocence, replacing it with a hum of fear and unworthiness. And unless that energy is transmuted—not just talked about but moved, expressed, released—it shapes every interaction with the body, with intimacy, with power.

Healing sexual trauma requires courage—the courage to look at what happened without minimizing it, the courage to name what was done without shame, the courage to face the truth that much of what we thought was "just who I am" was actually "how I survived."

Mental (Verbal) Abuse

Mental and verbal abuse is the ghost of trauma—the one that rarely gets named because it leaves no scars. But make no mistake: its wounds run deep. Words can become weapons sharper than knives, and when those words come from the mouths of those we love, they carve beliefs into the soft clay of the mind that harden over time into cages we can't see.

Mental abuse isn't just yelling. It's belittling. It's shaming. It's the constant drip of criticism that erodes a child's sense of worth until they stop trying to speak, stop trying to dream, stop believing they deserve more. It's the sarcasm disguised as humor, the guilt used as leverage, the control masked as "discipline." And generationally, this form of abuse is everywhere—because many of us were raised to believe that fear builds strength, that dominance equals love, that silence equals respect.

But here's the truth: yelling isn't guidance. Criticism isn't care. Control isn't love. These patterns didn't start with us—they were passed down like broken inheritance. Parents who were silenced learn to silence. Parents who were shamed learn to shame. Not because they're cruel, but because they've never known another way.

And here's where the nervous system comes in: constant verbal attack keeps the body in a low-grade state of threat. The child learns to anticipate tone shifts the way soldiers scan for enemy movement. They stop expressing to stay safe. They live with a hum of hypervigilance that follows them into every classroom, every workplace, every relationship. And like all trauma, this doesn't just live in thought—it lives in frequency. The vibration of mental abuse is contraction. It collapses confidence. It fractures coherence. It turns the voice inward until self-talk becomes a replica of the words that once broke us.

But here's the hope: what was learned can be unlearned. The voice that once cut can be softened. The energy that once contracted can expand. And when we name the pattern—without shame, without blame—we create the space for something new: the frequency of compassion, the vibration of truth, the resonance of love that doesn't hurt.

What Is Trauma?

So what is trauma, really?

Textbooks will tell you it's a deeply distressing or disturbing experience that overwhelms an individual's ability to cope, and while that definition isn't wrong, it's far too small to hold the truth of what trauma is and what it does. Trauma isn't just an event that happened—it's the echo of that event vibrating through the nervous system long after the moment has passed. It's not the knife—it's the wound. Not the memory—it's the imprint. Trauma is the fracture between who you are and who you were forced to become to survive.

It doesn't stay in the story. It lives in the body. It hides in the cells, in the fascia, in the subconscious patterns that feel like personality but are really adaptations. It lives in the breath you hold without realizing, in the shoulders that never drop, in the way you scan for danger even in safe rooms. Trauma is what happens when the body says, *I can't integrate this, so I'll store it.* And it stores it everywhere—in the spine, in the gut, in the field of energy that surrounds you like an invisible shield humming with unprocessed pain.

Every time you said "I'm fine" when you weren't, your nervous system kept the receipt. Every time you silenced what you felt, ignored what you needed, swallowed what you wanted to scream, the body filed it away. And those files don't disappear with time—they accumulate, like pressure behind a dam, until one day the dam can't hold anymore.

That day came for me after four decades of running on autopilot, of performing strength while carrying silence like a secret. My collapse didn't look like a breakdown from the outside. It looked like a panic attack that felt like death, hitting me out of nowhere, ripping the breath from my lungs, convincing me I was about to die. Three times in one week, I ended up in the ER, hooked up to machines, waiting for someone to tell me what was wrong. And when the doctor said, *You're fine—it's just anxiety,* something inside me shattered. Because what do you do when your body feels like it's dying and everyone tells you you're okay?

You listen. Finally.

What I didn't understand then but know now is that my body wasn't betraying me. It was saving me. It was dragging decades of unprocessed trauma into the light because carrying it any longer would have killed me. That's what I call the moment of singularity—the point where the nervous system says, *No more.* Where the energy you've compressed for years erupts like a volcano through symptoms—panic, insomnia, chest pain, intrusive thoughts—forcing you to face what you've avoided.

And here's the thing: trauma doesn't just create symptoms. It creates strategies. The hustle, the overgiving, the perfectionism, the addiction, the endless need to prove—they're all strategies to outrun the weight of what hasn't been felt. And those strategies work, until they don't. Until the collapse comes. Until your vibration, stretched to its limit, snaps and demands recalibration.

Because trauma isn't just psychological—it's physiological, neurological, and energetic. It reshapes the brain. It floods the body with cortisol, rewires the vagus nerve, and keeps the amygdala firing like a faulty alarm. But beyond the biology, it distorts your frequency. It pulls your energy field into contraction. It lowers your vibration to a hum of fear, shame, and hypervigilance. And that hum becomes the soundtrack of your life—shaping your choices, your relationships, your sense of self.

And here's the most devastating truth: trauma is rarely isolated to one lifetime. It's ancestral. Generational. It travels through epigenetic coding, through family dynamics, through the stories we never tell but always feel. The rage that erupts without warning, the panic that makes no sense, the shame you can't name—maybe they didn't start with you. Maybe they've been echoing through your bloodline for centuries, waiting for someone to say, *it ends here.*

So what is trauma? It's not just pain. It's the absence of integration. It's the rupture between truth and survival. It's the low-frequency hum that keeps you small, disconnected, and braced for impact long after the threat is gone.

But here's what trauma isn't: it isn't your identity. It isn't a life sentence. Trauma is not the full story—it's the chapter where you begin to wake up. Because every panic attack, every breakdown, every moment of collapse is a message: *Come back.* Come back to the body. Come back to the presence. Come back to the parts of yourself you left behind.

When trauma meets consciousness, everything changes. Not overnight. Not without discomfort. But awareness opens the door. And on the other side of that door is choice. Choice to stop running. Choice to stop abandoning yourself. Choice to stop vibrating at the frequency of survival and start resonating with life.

This chapter isn't about blame. It's about responsibility—the radical responsibility of saying, *I will no longer live as an echo of my past. I will no longer carry what isn't mine to carry. I will no longer abandon the self I was born to be.*

Because here's the truth: you didn't choose your wounds. But you can choose what happens next. And that choice—the choice to turn toward what hurts instead of away—is the beginning of the most sacred work you will ever do. The work of returning. The work of re-aligning. The work of reclaiming the vibration that was always yours before the world taught you to contract.

You are not your trauma.

You are the one becoming aware of it.

And awareness is the most powerful beginning there is.

Chapter Six
The 3 T's

> **"You must descend into yourself to rise beyond yourself — only by feeling it all can you become something new."**
>
> — *Edy Lopez*

Transmutation is not a straight line, and when you are in pain, when your chest feels like it might collapse from the weight of emotions you cannot name, the last thing on your mind will be the word "transmutation." In those moments, the only thing you will know is the ache. The heaviness. The feeling that life is pressing down on your bones, making every breath feel like a burden. There will be days when you feel 100 percent alone, like no one in this entire world could possibly understand the chaos within you. And truthfully, in those moments, it won't matter who tries to help because no words will make sense. You will not be able to explain what is happening, not to them, and not even to yourself. You will want to turn off the lights, bury yourself under the weight of blankets, and pretend the world does not exist. Everything in you will crave escape—silence, darkness, oblivion.

And this is the paradox: the more you try to numb, the louder the body becomes. The more you run, the harder the emotions chase you. This is why transmutation matters—because when the storm rages, and you are standing alone in the middle of the downpour with no map and no shelter, the only way out is through. You will have to meet yourself in the storm and trust that the destination you cannot yet see is not death, but rebirth. And yes, this will demand faith. Faith in something deeper than reason. Faith that the shaking in your hands and the pounding in your chest are not signs of failure—they are signs of release.

Transmutation is not a poetic theory. It is physics applied to the soul. Energy cannot be destroyed—it can only change form. This is not an idea; it is law. And trauma is energy. The moments you could not process—the neglect, the abuse, the abandonment—they didn't vanish when you buried them. They sank deeper, into the tissues, into the nervous system, into the architecture of your very breath. The body is the container of every unfinished story. And when it can no longer contain the weight, it erupts—not to punish you, but to free you.

Science calls this somatic release. The body does not speak in language—it speaks in movement. Crying, shaking, sweating, trembling—these are not breakdowns. These are breakthroughs. They are the body completing the survival response it once had to suppress. They are the nervous system saying, *I am ready to finish what began years ago.* This is what happened to me in the darkest nights of my life, when I collapsed on the floor, drenched in panic, heart racing so fast I thought it would burst. I thought I was dying, but what was dying was the illusion—the version of me that survived by holding everything in.

I didn't understand it then. I only knew that I wanted out. I wanted the pain to end, the storm to pass. I thought suicide was the only way to quiet the noise inside me. But looking back, I see the truth: I didn't want to die. I wanted to live—I just didn't know how. I wanted the weight gone. I wanted the lies gone. I wanted the masks gone. The death I craved was not the death of my body—it was the death of my false self. And that is exactly what transmutation is: the burning away of what no longer serves, so what is real can finally breathe.

The symptoms—suffocating breath, numb face, racing heart, trembling body—were not signs of sickness. They were signals of liberation. My nervous system, overloaded for decades, was finally releasing the energy it had been forced to store. And yes, it felt like hell. But that hell was my passageway to freedom.

Transmutation is where the alchemy begins—dense energy becoming lighter, vibration rising, frequency shifting. And here is why it matters beyond you: unhealed trauma is never personal. It is ancestral. It is generational. The patterns you carry—the rage, the silence, the shame—were handed to you by those who never had the chance to release them. When you begin to move that energy through breath, through sound, through movement, you are not just healing yourself. You are breaking chains that began long before your birth.

This is not a step to rush. It is not something to analyze from the safety of your intellect. It is something to feel. To surrender to. To trust. And when you do—when the sobs come without warning, when your body shakes as if possessed, when sound erupts from your throat like thunder—let it. Let the storm move through you because the storm is the healer. The pain is the purifier. This is transmutation: the moment you stop resisting the body and allow the energy to become what it always wanted to be—free.

And when the wave passes—and it will—you will notice a subtle shift. The ground feels steadier. The breath, deeper. The weight that once anchored you begins to lift. This is not the end of the journey, but it is the beginning of becoming.

Transcendence

Transcendence is the moment the fog begins to lift, not in a single, dramatic instant but in a series of quiet realizations that ripple through the mind like light filtering through the cracks of a long-closed door. If transmutation is the fire that burns through what no longer serves, then transcendence is the clear sky that emerges after the storm—the calm that allows you to see where you are, perhaps for the first time. It is the shift from merely surviving your pain to understanding it, not through the blunt instrument of logic alone, but through the soft precision of awareness. Through presence. Through waking up.

For years, I believed awareness meant thinking harder, analyzing more, stacking ideas like bricks to build a tower of certainty. But transcendence is not built—it is revealed. It is not about ascending to some ethereal place beyond the clouds, detaching from the grit of human life. It is not about spiritual bypass, pretending the wounds do not exist while wrapping them in words like "love and light." No—true transcendence is not an escape from humanity. It is the full embrace of it. It is about becoming radically present in the mess and beauty of existence while no longer being owned by the narratives that once defined you.

This is where the paradox deepens. Transcendence does not happen until after transmutation. You cannot think your way to liberation while the body still carries the weight of unprocessed pain. The nervous system must first discharge what it has stored in silence. Only then can the mind uncoil from its loops and glimpse the vastness that lies beyond its walls. This is the phase where you stop asking, "Why is this happening to me?" and begin to whisper, "What is this trying to teach me?" That single shift—subtle yet seismic—marks the beginning of awakening.

When you reach this space, something profound occurs: you become the witness. The observer of thoughts, patterns, and conditioned reactions. And this is not detachment born from numbness—it is clarity born from awareness. It is the ability to see the mind in motion without drowning in its currents. In neuroscience, this is called metacognition: the capacity to think about your thinking, to recognize that a thought is just a thought and not an unshakable truth. Psychology calls it cognitive reappraisal—the art of assigning new meaning to old pain. Spiritual traditions call it awakening. Different names for the same turning point: the moment you realize that your identity was never fixed. That the "you" you've been defending, protecting, justifying—might have been nothing more than a survival costume stitched together by trauma.

This is not a theory for me; it was lived. During my own unraveling—months of panic, sleepless nights, looping thoughts that clawed at the edges of my sanity—I had one revelation that changed everything: *I am not my thoughts.* They were loud, relentless, convincing, but they were not me. They were echoes of an old story, movie trailers playing on repeat, fragments of a script I did not have to keep performing. Transcendence began when I stopped reacting to those trailers and started watching them. When I understood that the mind was not the master but the messenger.

Science confirms what sages have long said: neurons that fire together wire together. This is neuroplasticity—**the brain's ability to reshape itself based on repetition and attention. When you practice observing rather than reacting, you carve new pathways in the brain.** You weaken the old circuits of fear and shame and strengthen the neural architecture of resilience and peace. Over time, the mind itself becomes an ally rather than an adversary. This is why transcendence is not a single, euphoric leap into enlightenment. It is a practice. A daily, moment-to-moment return to presence. It requires repetition. It requires grace. It requires breath.

And yet, transcendence is not just neurological. It is energetic. If transmutation raised your vibration by releasing emotional density, transcendence attunes the frequency of the mind. Thoughts carry charge. Every belief hums at a frequency. When your inner dialogue is steeped in shame, fear, and unworthiness, it sends out a resonance that shapes your reality to match. But as awareness deepens, those vibrations shift. Your thoughts, once heavy with judgment, begin to lighten. Your words soften. Your choices align with clarity rather than chaos. This is not metaphysical fantasy—it is coherence. Your inner state begins to harmonize with what you seek to create, and life responds in kind.

There is vulnerability here, of course. Awakening does not mean invincibility. You will still feel tender, still feel the ache of old habits calling you back. But now, you carry perspective. You meet your past self not with contempt but with compassion. You see that every coping mechanism, every shield of anger or silence, was once an act of survival. And survival, no matter how messy, is proof of resilience.

Here lies the sacred paradox of transcendence: it is not about killing the old self but integrating it, not about abandoning the shadow but inviting it into the light. For you are not just the clarity that emerges—you are also the chaos that shaped it. To transcend is not to become something other than human. It is to become fully human—with awareness, with depth, with the capacity to choose.

This is the threshold that prepares the soil for transformation. Because now, for the first time, you are not reacting—you are responding. You are not a prisoner of the past—you are the author of a future no longer bound by unconscious scripts.

You are no longer controlled by emotions or thoughts. Yes, you still have triggers, but you can see yourself clearly in those difficult moments and recover much faster. Your life is no longer determined by how you feel but by what your true calling is. You are neither the victim nor the victor in disagreements, because you've realized that you are no longer choosing sides. You have stepped out of the polarity of sides and can now see the whole picture.

This is transcendence: the mind awakening from its own illusions, aligning thought with truth, and stepping through the doorway into a life that feels entirely—and authentically—yours.

Transformation

Transformation is not a single moment of fireworks erupting in the sky. It is not the cinematic epiphany where everything suddenly falls into place and the world greets you with applause. No! Transformation is quieter, subtler, almost imperceptible at first. It is the slow unfolding of a new self, one decision at a time, one breath at a time, one thought at a time. If transmutation is the body's release and transcendence is the mind's awakening, then transformation is their union—the merging of body, mind, and spirit into a coherent harmony that becomes the foundation of your life.

Most people believe transformation happens through adding—adding new habits, new affirmations, new strategies. But real transformation is not about accumulation; it is about alignment. It is not becoming something new—it is remembering what you were before the world told you who to be. It is the slow, steady death of illusion until all that remains is what is real.

For years, I thought change was about doing more—reading more books, taking more courses, chasing the next method that promised freedom. But the truth is, transformation is not a strategy. It is a state. It is not a technique. It is a way of being. It is what happens when your choices are no longer made from fear or lack, when your words no longer drip with self-defense, when your actions no longer bow to shame. It is the day you wake up and realize that you are no longer fighting yourself. The war inside is over. That the voice that once screamed of unworthiness has gone quiet—not because it was silenced, but because it was integrated, seen, and understood.

And here is what makes transformation so profound: it does not simply change your habits. It changes the frequency with which those habits arise. You no longer force discipline through grit; you move with ease because your energy is no longer entangled in survival. You do not chase love or validation because you have dissolved the illusion of lack. This is why transformation cannot be faked. You can mimic the outer behavior for a season, but without the inner shift, the old patterns will return like shadows at dusk.

Science affirms what mystics have whispered for centuries: as you change your thoughts, you change your brain. Neuroplasticity—the brain's ability to rewire itself—is proof that the mind is not a fixed structure but a living system shaped by repetition and attention. Every time you choose presence over reaction, every time you interrupt an old pattern and create a new one, you carve a different pathway in the neural landscape. Over time, those pathways become highways, and what once felt like resistance becomes second nature.

But transformation is more than neural circuits—it is vibrational coherence. As your thoughts lighten, your emotional field stabilizes. Your nervous system, once trapped in cycles of fight or flight, begins to rest in safety. You stop leaking energy into a thousand directions and start channeling it with clarity. You become a tuning fork of alignment, your inner state resonating with the experiences you wish to create.

This is why, in transformation, life begins to mirror your inner reality. Opportunities that once seemed unreachable begin to arrive, not because the world changed, but because your frequency did.

This shift is not just personal—it is ancestral. When you transform, you end cycles that have lived for generations. The silence your mother carried, the rage your father swallowed, the shame your grandparents wore like armor—you refuse to pass these patterns forward. You become the interruption. The pivot point. The one who says, "It ends with me." And in doing so, you gift your children—and every life you touch—a different blueprint: a map drawn not by pain, but by presence.

For me, transformation came like dawn creeping over the mountains—slow, patient, almost unnoticed until one day the whole landscape was flooded with light. It followed the nights I thought I would not survive. It followed the panic attacks that left me curled on the floor, the numbness that stole the breath from my lungs, the despair that convinced me life had no meaning. It came after transmutation ripped open my body and after transcendence rewrote my mind. It came when I stopped fighting for control and started surrendering to the truth. Slowly, quietly, I began to notice the shifts. At first, they were so small I almost missed them—the way I could breathe without feeling the weight of dread pressing against my ribs, the way I could wake up without the echo of panic chasing me out of sleep, the way my mind, once a hurricane of uncontrollable thoughts, began to calm like waters after a storm. There was no celebration, no trumpet announcing my freedom. It was subtler than that—like dawn creeping over the mountains, spreading light across a valley that had known only shadow.

Transformation did not come in a single surge of clarity; it came in the ordinary moments. The way I said no when I used to say yes out of fear. The way I could sit in silence without drowning in it. The way joy began to feel possible again—not as a sudden burst, but as a slow return, like blood flowing back into numb limbs. Each decision, each breath, each act of presence became evidence that I was no longer the man I used to be.

And this is the essence of transformation: it does not erase the past, but it rearranges your relationship with it. The wounds remain, but they no longer define you. The memories live on, but they no longer own you. Where there was chaos, there is coherence. Where there was fragmentation, there is wholeness. This is not magic; it is the natural consequence of alignment—of energy reorganizing, of neural pathways rewiring, of vibration stabilizing at a higher frequency than before.

Science calls it neuroplasticity, the ability of the brain to reconfigure itself through new experiences, new thoughts, new behaviors. Energy science calls it coherence, the synchronizing of the heart and mind until they hum at the same rhythm. Spiritual wisdom calls it awakening—the point at which your being is no longer governed by fear but animated by truth. Different names, one reality: you become someone who no longer reacts from the wounds of the past but responds from the wisdom of the present.

Transformation, for me, was not about becoming someone else. It was about remembering who I have always been beneath the survival patterns, beneath the layers of conditioning, beneath the false self that life taught me to perform. And when that remembrance came—not in a roar, but in a whisper—it brought with it a power no external force could give: the power to live as myself, unapologetically, fully, and freely.

And so I say to you: do not look for transformation in the grand gestures. It hides in the subtle, in the consistent, in the moments you choose truth over fear, presence over distraction, surrender over control. It comes like dawn—not suddenly, but surely. And when it arrives, the whole landscape of your life will look different, not because the world changed, but because you did.

This is the work. This is the gift. This is transformation—the quiet revolution that begins inside and ripples outward into everything you touch.

The main thing I want you to understand about transformation is the impact it will have on your life—if you do the work. Not the work of pretending, not the work of performing, but the internal work of radical honesty, self-confrontation, and surrender. I am not a fan of developing three-step formulas or ten-step strategies, because in my lived experience, and in the lives of those who have walked through fire and come out transformed, I have found that nothing about life is linear. Life spirals. It loops. It returns to places we thought we'd left behind, not to punish us—but to show us what we missed the first time.

Still, just as water is composed of two hydrogen atoms and one oxygen—each playing an irreplaceable role in its structure—transformation, too, is a system. Not a rigid one, but an intelligent one. A system made of essential components that work synergistically to support healing, awakening, and alignment. The purpose of transformation is not simply to feel better, look better, or achieve more, but to understand this system deeply. And that system, in its simplest form, is composed of two dynamic forces: transmutation and transcendence.

Transmutation is the movement and alchemy of energy through the body. It is the release, the somatic surrender, the literal shifting of vibration and density. It's what happens when you cry and don't know why. When you scream into a pillow and feel thirty years of silence crack, it is the physical purification—the body letting go of what it was never meant to carry. Transcendence, on the other hand, is the mental and energetic process—the rising above the stories, the labels, the scripts we inherited. It is what happens when awareness enters the room, when the mind is no longer enslaved by the survival program of fear and shame. Together, these two processes form the gateway to real transformation.

And what is transformation, really? It's not about becoming something new—it's about returning to something ancient within you. Healing is the natural result of this return. When we stop striving to become someone, and instead release everything we are not, we begin to experience a profound homecoming. A recalibration. An inner restoration that moves through our cells like light reentering a long-abandoned room. We begin to feel new, not because we added something—but because we finally let go. We divorced the old versions of ourselves, not in hatred, but in love. We made space for the original self—the one that existed before the pain, before the programming, before the persona.

We must remember: transformation is not about self-improvement. It is about self-remembrance. The illusion of self-improvement in modern culture has become another form of egoism, dressed in spiritual language. Becoming the "best version" of yourself is not a matter of acquisition. It is not about how much knowledge you can gather, how many degrees you can collect, or how optimized your life becomes. There is no version of you out there that is waiting to be created. There is only the version of you that is waiting to be revealed once the noise is cleared. Yes, physical wealth and success can absolutely be part of this—but we must ask: is what I'm building an expression of my soul, or a compensation for my wound? If trauma is driving the train, even a beautiful destination will feel empty. And if that's the case, then pause. See it. Thank it. Love yourself through it. And keep going.

The soul of transformation, its deepest intention, is not to help you escape who you are—but to help you embody it. Fully. Authentically. And to do so in such a way that your very presence becomes a permission slip for others to heal. You see, the hero's journey is never complete until the hero returns—not to boast about the treasures found, but to light the way for those still walking through the dark. David Goggins embodies this in a way few people ever do. He doesn't speak often—but when he does, people listen, not because of charisma, but because of truth. He confronts the darkest corners of his past and invites us to do the same. He doesn't sugarcoat reality—he demands honesty, with yourself and with the mirror. "If you're fat, say it. If you're broke, say it." And this also includes if you were abused, abandoned, or neglected. Not to shame, but to liberate. That's the beginning of conscious awareness: calling things what they are. Naming the pain. Owning the truth. Forgiving the past. And then moving forward—not in victimhood, but in awakened responsibility.

My intention in writing this book is not to give you more tools to build better armor. The world has enough of that. My aim is to help you dissolve the armor altogether—through understanding, awareness, and the sacred discomfort of waking up. Transformation is not about remembering facts or chasing mountaintop enlightenment. It is not a fleeting "aha" moment or a spiritual badge. It is a deep, often disorienting process of self-realization. The kind that asks: What shaped me? Who did I become to survive? When did I lose myself? And how can I return?

This path is not reserved for monks, mystics, or motivational speakers. It is not for the few—it is for the many. For everyone. Whether you're wealthy or struggling, educated or uneducated, an entrepreneur or incarcerated—this process belongs to you. It is about your nervous system. Your thoughts. Your breath. Your ability to respond to life from love instead of fear. Transformation is the daily, often invisible choice to live from consciousness rather than ego. From creation instead of reaction. From love instead of survival.

And sometimes, transformation is nothing more than the courage to start again—when all odds are against you, when you've lost everything, and when the world feels like it has forgotten your name. It is the choice to look into the ashes and still believe in the fire within.

Chapter Seven
Planning

> **"The harder you try to control life, the less control you have."**
>
> — *Taoist Teaching*

Now that you understand the different types of trauma—what they are, how they show up, and how they've shaped your life—and now that you've seen how energy, vibration, and frequency all play a role in your body, your nervous system, and your identity… and now that you've walked through the fire of transmutation, touched the sky through transcendence, and tasted the truth of transformation—it's time.

It's time to live.

This isn't the kind of living where you go back to "normal." No. That version of life is gone, and it needs to be gone, because the self you were before awakening was built inside the architecture of survival, built from patterns you didn't choose, and often inherited from generations who also didn't know they had a choice. If you've made it this far, you already know—there's no going back. You've awakened. And whether your awakening happened through grief, illness, panic, trauma, or something sacred and spontaneous, this chapter is for the part of you that is asking: What now?

Living after awakening is about integration. It's not just about recognizing what you've been through; it's about turning those experiences into actions that shape your life every single day. Because knowledge without application remains static, and healing without structure can dissolve into memory rather than becoming a movement that carries you forward. This part of the journey requires grounded action, not the frantic action of survival, but the calm and intentional kind that honors what you have learned and creates conditions for you to keep expanding. Awareness is not enough anymore. Transformation means nothing if it doesn't touch your calendar, your habits, your mindset, your relationships, and your purpose. The shift you experienced—whether subtle or seismic—must now root itself in the soil of your daily existence, or else it risks becoming another distant echo of insight rather than the embodied presence of change.

And that's where planning comes in.

Planning as Conscious Creation

Planning is often misunderstood as control, but true planning—sacred planning—is not about constricting life into rigid timelines or orchestrating every detail as if uncertainty is the enemy. It is about building an internal and external environment that nurtures the frequency you've chosen to live in. Because life, by its very nature, will always invite chaos. It will hand you uncertainty. It will test the strength of your inner structure by removing the outer scaffolding you used to rely on. And if you do not have a blueprint—if you have not designed rhythms that serve your peace—you will default to the architecture of your old identity. You will slip back into the gravity of unconscious loops, those invisible cycles powered by memory and emotion that keep repeating themselves because that is what the brain does best: it predicts based on the past.

Your nervous system, by design, seeks familiarity. Familiarity equals safety, even when that familiarity is dysfunction, scarcity, or self-sabotage. Neuroscience tells us that the brain operates largely on predictive coding, meaning it doesn't simply react to the present—it anticipates based on prior experience, then filters reality to fit those expectations. So when you wake up each morning, if nothing interrupts the cycle, you will unconsciously repeat yesterday's emotions, yesterday's vibration, and yesterday's identity, even while consciously craving a different life. That is why insight without structure fails. That is why awakening alone is not liberation. The mind does not honor revelations without repetition, and the nervous system does not stabilize in safety without deliberate practice.

Planning is that practice.

It is the act of translating your highest awareness into daily behavior. It is the quiet rebellion against generational patterns that taught you to live reactively rather than creatively. It is saying: I will not wait for life to happen to me. I will choose the frequency I live in before the world makes that choice for me. Because if you do not choose your vibration, your vibration will default to the sum of unprocessed memories, ancestral fear, and cultural noise.

The Sacred Science of Mornings

This is why the morning matters so much. Before the world reaches for you—before notifications pull at your mind, before the opinions of others hijack your nervous system—there is a window of pure possibility. Neurobiology calls this the hypnopompic state, that brief stretch of time between sleep and wakefulness when the brain lingers in alpha and theta waves, those same slow rhythms that meditation cultivates. The first hour is a gateway to your subconscious, and the way you spend it has the power to shape the course of your entire day. If you enter that space with intention, you condition your nervous system toward coherence rather than chaos. If you squander it on autopilot, you hand over the pen to yesterday's story.

For me, this became non-negotiable after my collapse. When I say collapse, I mean the months of panic attacks that stripped me of every illusion of control, the nights I thought my heart would give out, the ER visits that ended with nothing but sedatives and hollow reassurances that I was "fine." I was not fine. My body was screaming what my mind had ignored for decades. That crisis was the doorway to awakening, but awakening was not the finish line. It was the starting point for rebuilding a life that would not drag me back into the abyss I barely survived. And the first brick in that foundation was my morning routine.

I began waking up at 5:00 AM, sometimes 6:00 if my body needed more rest, because those early hours carried a stillness that felt like medicine. Before sunrise, the world is quiet, and that quiet holds a frequency—a resonance of possibility unpolluted by the day's demands. I would begin with breathwork, not as a trendy ritual but as a neurological reset. Deep, rhythmic breathing stimulates the vagus nerve, activating the parasympathetic nervous system, the branch of your biology responsible for rest, repair, and safety. This matters because trauma wires the body for hypervigilance; it locks you in fight-or-flight, a state where presence is impossible because the body believes danger is imminent. Breathwork interrupts that loop.

It lowers cortisol. It slows the heartbeat. It whispers to the body: We are safe now.

After breath came meditation. Not the performative kind, not the ten minutes squeezed in while scrolling notifications, but a full immersion into stillness—a surrender to silence that felt both foreign and familiar. Meditation reshapes the brain. Studies in neuroplasticity show that consistent meditation thickens the prefrontal cortex (linked to focus and decision-making) and shrinks the amygdala (the fear center). In other words, it physically rewires the pathways that once imprisoned you in panic. For me, meditation was not optional. It was survival. It was how I gained the first sense of control after months of drowning in terror that had no name.

Only after breath and meditation did I reach for the pen. I would write—not essays, not polished paragraphs, but raw plans. Questions first: What matters today? What vibration do I choose? Then answers: small steps, intentional choices, boundaries. This is not a productivity culture. This is a vibrational strategy. Because the plan is not about cramming hours with tasks, it is about creating alignment between your energy and your actions, so your life reflects the self you fought to become.

Why Morning Structure Breaks Generational Cycles

It might seem personal, but this is bigger than you. This is generational work. Many of us were raised in households where mornings were chaos—where the day began in reactivity, where stress was inherited before breakfast. That becomes a blueprint encoded in the nervous system and, through epigenetics, it becomes a thread in the fabric of generational trauma. Planning a calm, intentional morning is not just self-care—it is ancestral repair. You are interrupting centuries of survival mode by teaching your body a new pattern, and when you embody that, you offer that pattern to those who come after you. This is why planning matters. Because unplanned lives tend to repeat the pain of their predecessors, and planned lives—when rooted in presence—tend to birth futures where peace is possible.

The Blueprint Beyond the Morning

Planning does not end with sunrise. The morning is the anchor, but the day is the expression. This is where you extend that vibration into practical rhythms: meals that nourish rather than numb, conversations that align rather than drain, work that serves rather than enslaves. Your calendar becomes a mirror of your consciousness. It becomes a container strong enough to hold the frequency you've chosen when life begins to test you—which it will. And when challenges arise, you won't collapse into chaos, because you've built a nervous system rooted in stillness and a mind that trusts the blueprint it created in the quiet hours of dawn.

Planning is the bridge between inner transformation and outer expression. You've rebuilt your house from the inside—now it's time to furnish it with people, ideas, actions, and rhythms that match the new you. This is not about perfection. It's about alignment. It's about living a life that reflects what you've healed, what you've seen, and who you've become. It's about growing the sprout that just broke through the dirt, seeking to girth its roots and, for one day, to become the tree for others to lean on. And in doing so, you not only heal yourself—you interrupt generational trauma by refusing to pass on unconsciousness disguised as tradition.

Living

Living is not about waiting for everything to be perfect. It's about embracing what is—right now, as it is, without editing reality to match your fantasies or contorting your soul to fit someone else's narrative of success. After all the healing, after all the shedding and awakening, there comes a moment where the deepest work is not in doing more, but in simply being present. And that is harder than it sounds, because presence feels simple in theory, but for those of us who have lived decades in survival mode, stillness feels like a threat, and allowing life to move without gripping the wheel feels like surrendering to danger. This is the paradox: the place you long for—the ease, the peace, the flow—exists only on the other side of letting go of control, and yet your entire nervous system has been conditioned to equate control with safety. So yes, living after awakening is both art and science. It is not passive, but it is not frantic either. It is the delicate, daily practice of grounding your awareness in the present moment, not as a spiritual slogan but as a biological necessity for coherence and a vibrational doorway to everything you once thought was outside of you.

Too many of us spend years, even decades, in hypervigilance, clinging to control as if the universe is plotting against us, constantly bracing for impact, always preparing for the next blow because experience taught us that pain is predictable and joy is fragile. We over-plan, over-perform, overcompensate for the chaos of our past, and then wonder why our nervous system never relaxes, why love feels unsafe, why abundance feels unreachable, why stillness feels unbearable. Healing eventually brings you to a place where the only thing left to do… is live. Fully. Honestly. Freely. But that freedom requires trust, and trust is impossible in a body that has never been taught how to feel safe without controlling the external world. This is why living is a discipline. It is not the absence of action. It is not apathy or avoidance. It is the conscious act of choosing presence even when fear seduces you back into old survival patterns.

Living in the now is not some mystical idea reserved for gurus and monks—it is neuroscience and physiology. The body cannot exist anywhere but the present. It breathes now. It digests now. It feels now. But the mind—left unchecked—lives in a time machine. It drags you back into the gravity of old memories or catapults you forward into imagined disasters, and every time it does, your nervous system responds as if those illusions are real. That is why anxiety spikes and panic hijack your breath. Your body cannot tell the difference between a memory and a current event if your mind is fully immersed in that memory. This is why presence is medicine. When you anchor in the now, when you feel the breath in your lungs, the earth beneath your feet, the pulse in your hands, you send a signal to your nervous system that says: We are here. We are safe. We can stop fighting ghosts.

The moment you stop trying to control every detail of your life, the moment you trust that the universe is not out to punish you, is the moment life begins to unfold for you—not against you. It is the space where you become a participant in the dance rather than the choreographer of every move. And that matters, because control—despite its illusion of power—operates on a low vibration of fear. Flow, on the other hand, resonates with trust, and trust amplifies coherence across every level of your being: mental, emotional, energetic, even cellular. When you live in flow, your brain shifts into alpha and low beta rhythms, the same states associated with creativity and relaxed focus. Your body moves from sympathetic dominance (fight-or-flight) into parasympathetic balance. Stress hormones decline. Dopamine rises—not from the addictive spikes of instant gratification, but from the sustained reward of meaningful engagement. Your energy stops scattering across infinite "what ifs" and gathers into the singular frequency of now, and that is where life feels lighter, because you are no longer vibrating in opposition to reality.

When I lost my job as a teacher after two and a half years—one of over 500 staff members laid off—it would have been easy to spiral. In the past, I would've panicked. My nervous system would've gone straight into fight-or-flight. I would've drowned in anxiety, questioning everything, blaming everything. I know that spiral because I've lived it, the racing thoughts, the tight chest, the body convinced it's on the brink of death even while logic insists otherwise. It's the same current that pulled me into months of panic attacks after my breakdown, the same darkness that nearly seduced me into ending my life when the pain felt endless. And that memory was still in my body the day I opened that email announcing the layoff. But here's the difference: this time, I stayed present. This time, the practices I had cultivated—those quiet mornings of breath and stillness—rose up like a shield between me and the chaos. Yes, I became emotional. Yes, the emotion was real. But I didn't unravel. I didn't let the old versions of me take the wheel. Because I had built an inner architecture strong enough to withstand the external collapse. I knew—deep in my bones—that life was giving me a doorway. An opening. And the moment I stepped through it, I saw what it was: a chance to live what I had been writing about. A chance to walk in alignment with everything I now know. A chance to live at the frequency I had fought to reach.

Because the point of awakening is not to become holy, it's to become whole.

Living in this new way is about applying the plan you've created—not as a rigid system, but as a living, breathing guide. It's about staying awake to the subtle movements of your energy, because energy whispers before it screams, and if you listen early, you don't have to be blindsided by breakdowns. It's about choosing peace over panic, presence over prediction, and alignment over approval. The plan gives you structure, but living gives you soul. One is the form, the other is the flow. Together, they form the dance of divine embodiment, and that dance will look different every day because life is not static, and neither are you.

And yes, it takes courage. Because life won't always go your way, plans will fall apart. People will leave. Money will run low. Opportunities will slip through your hands. Old triggers will resurface when you least expect them. But even then—even in all that—you are still being held. You are still exactly where you need to be to grow, because the measure of awakening is not whether the storm stops; it is whether you remain anchored when it comes. To live is to trust and remember that this moment is the only one guaranteed. You don't have to be perfect; you just have to be present. And when you are, the universe responds—not always with what you want, but with what you need.

So breathe into it. Let life touch you. Let the wind remind you that you are still here. Let the loss remind you that you're still in motion. Let every change be your teacher. And let the moment you're in be your greatest miracle. Living is not a destination. It's the dance you do while everything else unfolds.

And here's something I want to speak to directly—because I've lived it. Living in the present isn't always as smooth as it sounds, especially after awakening. I know that it is much easier said than done, and returning to myself to live was quite difficult. The part of me that held me back from living was the fear of making the same mistakes again. But I realized that this was the same fear I had before, only now I had the tools to move forward. I have to admit it was not easy at the beginning because the whole experience of awakening was traumatic enough. Traumatic from the perspective that it was new and that I had to go through so many stages—breaking down the scaffolding of my old identity, surrendering the armor that once kept me alive, learning to trust a reality I could not predict. But eventually, the universe pushed me left, right, backwards, and forward, and I saw that the new version of myself had captained the ship, steering not by fear but by faith.

Living is remembering that no moment is wasted, no detour is final, and no ending is truly an end. It is learning to let the rhythm of life become your rhythm without losing your center. And in that rhythm, you discover what freedom really is—not the absence of uncertainty, but the presence of unwavering trust.

Recovering

Recovery is the breath after the breakthrough. It's the pause between heartbeats, the sacred silence after the roar. Transformation often announces itself with fire—with panic or epiphany, with tears that feel like rivers and revelations that shake your bones. But recovery? Recovery moves like water. Gentle. Patient. Persistent. It does not demand attention, yet it determines whether the changes you fought for will take root or fade back into memory. And this is the part almost no one talks about, because our culture worships the drama of beginnings and the glory of endings, but overlooks the quiet, repetitive work in the middle—the work of integration.

After you awaken, after you shatter the illusions that held you hostage for years, after you peel away the layers of inherited pain and rewire the mind that once betrayed you, there comes a moment when the world expects you to sprint into your new life. But your nervous system has other plans. It needs time. It needs rhythm. It needs proof that the danger is gone and that safety is not a fleeting visitor but a permanent resident. Because awakening, as liberating as it feels in spirit, is traumatic for the body. It dismantles old systems, and what follows is a biological and energetic recalibration—a returning home that does not happen overnight.

Recovery is not a luxury. It is not indulgence. It is a necessity. When the sympathetic nervous system has been in overdrive for decades—when fight-or-flight was your default—switching into parasympathetic balance does not happen by wishing it so. It happens through repetition, through practices that signal safety, through choices that whisper to the body: It's okay now. We're not running anymore. That's why recovery often feels like doing nothing, but in that "nothing," everything is happening. In the stillness, cortisol levels drop. In the breath, heart rate variability improves. In the pause, the brain shifts from survival circuitry into repair mode. This is science, not sentiment.

For me, recovery began with rest, but it did not end there. At first, I thought stillness meant lying in bed for hours, and in the early days after my breakdown, that was true—I could barely move without triggering another wave of panic. But as my body healed, recovery became active. It became a conscious choice to slow down, not because I was weak, but because strength built on exhaustion collapses eventually. I had to learn that productivity without alignment is another form of self-abandonment, and I had done enough of that in my old life. So I listened. I made my mornings non-negotiable. Breathwork. Meditation. Planning. Then, I layered in new rhythms—gentle movement, mindful eating, deep hydration, and fasting. Later, I explored modalities that helped accelerate the body's repair process—not as a quick fix, but as an investment in the nervous system I had nearly destroyed.

Recovery is unique for everyone, but the principles remain universal: rest, nourish, move, recalibrate, repeat. It is cyclical, not linear. Some days, recovery will look like stillness. Other days, it will look like sweat or laughter, or nature. But all of it matters, because without recovery, you risk collapsing into the very burnout that awakening delivered you from. And if you're not careful, you will interpret that collapse as failure rather than what it really is: feedback that you bypassed the most essential phase of transformation.

Here is the truth: without recovery, the old self returns dressed in new clothes. Unhealed patterns resurface. Panic seeps through the cracks. For me, that almost happened. There were weeks after my awakening when I thought, I'm better now. I'm unstoppable. I started working fifteen-hour days again, chasing new dreams with old habits, until my body pulled the emergency brake and panic whispered, Did you really think you could outrun me? That was my reminder. Healing is not an event. It is a lifestyle. And recovery is the ground that lifestyle grows from.

So, what does recovery look like beyond the abstract? Yes, it's breath and meditation. Yes, it's saying no without guilt, reclaiming boundaries, and allowing yourself to be. But it's also embracing tools and modalities that support the biology of safety and the energy of coherence. Below are some of the most effective practices and therapies I've integrated into my own life and recommended to others navigating the delicate terrain between awakening and embodiment:

Recovery Modalities for the Nervous System and Energy Recalibration

- Meditation

A cornerstone practice for nervous system regulation and mental clarity, meditation lowers cortisol, increases gray matter density in the prefrontal cortex, and reduces the size of the amygdala—the brain's fear center. Consistent practice rewires neural pathways, improves focus, and strengthens emotional resilience. Energetically, meditation raises your vibration by aligning thought, breath, and awareness in coherence.

- Breath-work

Conscious breathing patterns, such as diaphragmatic breathing or box breathing, activate the parasympathetic nervous system and improve vagal tone, which directly calms stress responses. Breath-work regulates oxygen and carbon dioxide balance, stabilizes heart rate variability, and grounds the mind in the present moment. On an energetic level, breath is the carrier of life force (prana), making this practice essential for clearing stagnant energy and restoring inner harmony.

- Fasting & Intermittent Fasting

Fasting allows the body to rest and repair. It activates autophagy—your body's natural cellular detox process—and helps reduce inflammation, regulate blood sugar, and reset the nervous system. Intermittent fasting, such as eating within an 8-hour window and fasting for 16 hours, is a gentle, sustainable practice that sharpens mental clarity and calms emotional reactivity. Even 12–14 hours without food overnight can support deep healing. More than physical, fasting is energetic—it clears space, quiets noise, and invites stillness. In that stillness, you realign with your body's natural rhythm and tune your frequency to presence.

- Yoga

Yoga is more than movement—it is breath, awareness, and alignment. Through gentle postures and intentional breathing, yoga soothes the nervous system, increases vagal tone, and helps discharge trapped emotional energy stored in the body. Whether practiced for 10 minutes in silence or in a full flow, yoga grounds you in the present and opens pathways for energy to move. It restores balance, raises vibration, and reconnects you with the wisdom your body has carried all along.

- Infrared Sauna

Infrared heat penetrates deep into muscles and tissues, helping the body release toxins, reduce inflammation, and relax the nervous system. As the body sweats, stagnant energy moves, the parasympathetic system activates, and breath deepens.

Just 20–30 minutes a few times per week can improve circulation, calm the mind, and reset your internal rhythm.

- Russian Vañas (Steam Bath + Cold Plunge)

The Russian banya, a ritual of heat, steam, and sudden cold, awakens the body and purifies the nervous system. The cycle of hot steam followed by cold immersion creates a deep vascular flush—improving circulation, reducing inflammation, and stimulating the lymphatic system. But it's more than physical—it's ancestral. A ritual of release. A reminder that through pressure and contrast, resilience is born.

- Cryotherapy (Cold Therapy)

Exposing the body to extreme cold (via ice baths or cryo chambers) reduces inflammation, boosts endorphins, and strengthens stress resilience by training the nervous system to stay calm under pressure. Regular cold exposure improves circulation and can reset the body's stress response, making it a powerful ally for trauma recovery.

- Massage Therapy

Touch is medicine for the nervous system. Massage reduces muscular tension, but more importantly, it stimulates the vagus nerve, increases oxytocin (the bonding hormone), and signals safety to a body that associates touch with threat. It rewires trust through sensation.

- PEMF Therapy (Pulsed Electromagnetic Field)

PEMF devices deliver low-frequency electromagnetic waves that restore cellular energy and improve mitochondrial function. Think of it as recharging your body's batteries—essential after years of energy depletion from chronic stress.

- Red Light Therapy

Exposure to red and near-infrared light enhances cellular repair, reduces inflammation, and improves mood by stimulating mitochondrial function and boosting ATP production. It's a science-backed way to restore vitality at the cellular level.

- Sunlight Exposure (10–15 Minutes Daily)

Natural sunlight resets circadian rhythms, enhances serotonin production, and regulates melatonin for better sleep. Morning sunlight, in particular, anchors your biological clock and stabilizes mood, which is crucial after years of dysregulation caused by trauma and stress.

- Mild Hyperbaric Oxygen Therapy (mHBOT)

This therapy involves breathing concentrated oxygen in a pressurized chamber, increasing oxygen delivery to tissues and accelerating cellular repair. It reduces inflammation, promotes neurogenesis (the creation of new neurons), and enhances energy production—especially beneficial for those recovering from neurological stress, trauma, or chronic fatigue.

Each of these modalities works differently, but all share one common purpose: to create coherence between mind, body, and energy by restoring balance at the most fundamental levels of biology and frequency. They are not shortcuts, but they are powerful accelerators. When combined with mindful living—breath, meditation, conscious movement—they create a foundation strong enough to carry you into the life you are building, not as a performance, but as an authentic embodiment of peace.

Recovery is where transformation becomes sustainable. It is where you learn to live without rushing, to create without forcing, to move without fear. It is the slow alchemy of rest and rhythm, the unseen work that holds the seen world together. Do not skip it. Do not minimize it. Honor it as the sacred bridge between who you were and who you are becoming.

Chapter Eight
Breath

> **"When I let go of what I am, I become what I might be."**
>
> — *Lao Tzu*

The most vital thing we do. The very first thing we did when we entered this world, and the last thing we'll do when we leave. Yet somehow, in the middle of all that living, we forget how to do it. Not mechanically—we breathe whether we think about it or not. But consciously, intentionally, and powerfully.

And maybe that's because breath is so automatic, so woven into the fabric of being, that we mistake it for something ordinary when in reality it is the most extraordinary thread connecting life to life, moment to moment, self to self. Every inhale is an invitation and every exhale a surrender, a constant dance between taking in and letting go. Breath is not simply air moving through lungs; it is rhythm, it is music, it is the silent conductor of the nervous system. It keeps time for the body's orchestra, guiding when to expand and when to release, when to move into alertness, and when to fall back into calm. Breath is the bridge between the unconscious and conscious mind, the hidden key to the doors most of us forgot even existed.

And when life spins us into chaos—when the mind races, the body tightens, and the heart feels like it's carrying a hundred-pound weight—breath is the only thing that can bring us back. But here's what most people don't know: the way you breathe tells the story of your life. That sentence is not metaphorical. It is a scientific truth and a spiritual truth intertwined.

*****So let's pause for a few seconds. Take a deep breath and exhale for a long 10 seconds*****

If you breathe shallow, fast, or hold your breath often, it's not just a habit. It's a memory. It's your body's way of adapting to danger that may no longer be present but still lives inside your cells like an echo.

Maybe that danger came years ago. Maybe it was a parent yelling in a kitchen where walls felt like they were closing in. Maybe it was war. Maybe it was heartbreak or a hospital visit or a betrayal you never healed from. Whatever it was, your breath remembered.

And here's the part we rarely consider: sometimes that memory didn't even start with you. We inherit the breath of those who raised us. If your mother lived in a constant state of anxiety, if your father carried unresolved rage, if generations before you lived through famine, migration, oppression, or loss, their nervous systems adapted in order to survive—and breath was part of that adaptation. Fast forward decades later, and you might be wondering why your chest feels tight even in safe spaces. This is why: breath carries lineage. It is both deeply personal and profoundly ancestral.

From a scientific perspective, breath directly affects the autonomic nervous system, which governs your stress response. There are two main branches: the sympathetic nervous system (your fight-or-flight response) and the parasympathetic nervous system (your rest-and-digest mode). When you inhale, your sympathetic system activates slightly. When you exhale slowly, you engage the parasympathetic system. Which means: when you lengthen and slow your exhale, you are literally signaling safety to your body. You are teaching your system that it is safe to return home.

***** So let's pause again for a few seconds. Take a deep breath, hold for 5 seconds (5, 4, 3, 2, & 1), and exhale for a long 10 seconds (10, 9, 8, 7, 6, 5, 4, 3, 2, & 1). If you felt dizzy, amazing! *****

Let me say that again because it's that important: you can teach your nervous system to feel safe again—just by breathing. And if we go deeper, we find that this teaching happens not just on the level of muscle or nerve, but on the level of energy. Every inhale draws in not only oxygen but subtle vibrational patterns that influence the entire electromagnetic field surrounding your body. Every exhale is an opportunity to discharge static—old tension, trapped memory, the dense energy of grief or fear that never had a way out. This is why people sob uncontrollably during breath-work sessions without anyone saying a word: because the body keeps the score, and breath knows how to read it.

But here's the paradox: the people who need breath-work the most are usually the ones who've forgotten how to breathe deeply. That was me. I didn't know I was holding my breath until life forced me to exhale. It happened during my panic attacks. It happened during my awakening. My chest tightened. My breaths became short, panicked, and shallow. I thought I was dying. But what was really happening? My nervous system was trying to release decades of stored trauma.

I remember moments—sitting alone, crying, even screaming. And then, suddenly, breath would return. A deep inhale would rise like a wave. An exhale would fall like surrender. It was during these moments—raw, unfiltered—that I realized healing wasn't about fixing anything. It was about feeling everything. And breath was my gateway.

Breath-work became a practice. Sometimes gentle. Sometimes intense. There were times I used box breathing—inhale for four, hold for four, exhale for four, hold again. It calmed and regulated me. Other times, I did conscious connected breathing—a method where the inhale and exhale flow without pause. That cracked me wide open. There were days I'd cry. Others where I'd laugh. Some sessions felt like soul surgery. But every time, something moved. Something shifted.

From Emergency Rooms to Emotional Resurrection

I never expected breath to save my life. Not in the poetic sense—but in the real, raw, paramedics-and-panic-attack kind of way. At the time, I had quit my job, was in the middle of a divorce, and my nervous system was collapsing after decades of white-knuckling through life. I didn't know it then, but the mask I had been wearing—strong, capable, always in control—was cracking, and everything I had refused to feel was rushing to the surface.

It started with the panic attacks. At first, I thought they were random—brief moments of terror, heart pounding, chest tightening—but they came like storms I couldn't predict or control. Then came the ER visits.

Three times in one week. Each time I was sure: *this is it, I'm dying.*

I remember the first one vividly. My chest felt like a vice was squeezing the air out of me, my arms tingled, and my legs went numb. My mind screamed *heart attack* as I gripped the steering wheel and somehow made it to the hospital. Fluorescent lights. The antiseptic smell. Nurses rushing me onto a bed, attaching wires, EKG monitors beeping like mechanical heartbeats, doctors asking questions I couldn't answer because all I could think was: *I can't breathe.*

They ran every test. Blood work. EKGs. Monitors. Over and over, the same words: "You're fine." But I wasn't fine. I was unraveling. My body was in full revolt, my mind spinning into existential chaos, and the system that had carried me through years of stress and trauma had finally broken down.

What I didn't know then—but I know now—is that panic isn't random. It's not a weakness. It's not a glitch. It's the body's last desperate attempt to release what the mind refuses to process. All the trauma I had buried, every emotion I had silenced, every night I held my breath through arguments, deployments, heartbreaks—was still living inside me. Energy doesn't disappear. It waits. And when the weight becomes unbearable, it explodes through the nervous system like a storm breaking a dam.

That's what was happening to me. Decades of unprocessed emotion vibrating in my cells at a frequency so dense it was pulling me under. This is what trauma does: it traps you in survival mode, and survival mode rewires your breath. Shallow, rapid inhales. Tight chest. Locked diaphragm. And because breath is the metronome of the nervous system, when the rhythm goes off, the whole orchestra falls apart.

The ER couldn't fix that. No test could measure what was happening on the level of energy, vibration, or memory. What I needed wasn't medication. I needed to teach my body that it was safe to breathe again. I needed to exhale.

After my third ER visit, something in me clicked. The doctors kept telling me I was fine. But I knew I wasn't fine. I wasn't living—I was bracing for impact every moment of every day, waiting for the next wave of panic. And then came the invitation. My sister said, "Go to this breath-work event." I almost laughed.

After what I had just been through, how could breathing fix anything?

But something deep inside me whispered: *Go.*

I walked into this large ballroom with a hundred other souls, probably seeking healing as well, but I was still vibrating with residual panic. The space was dimly lit, mats laid out in a circle, soft music playing. I lay down, my body rigid, my mind scanning for danger like it always did. The facilitator spoke calmly, explaining the technique—conscious connected breathing, a circular rhythm with no pause between inhale and exhale. It sounded simple. But nothing about what followed was simple.

At first, it felt awkward. Mechanical. My jaw clenched. My chest resisted. My thoughts screamed, "This is stupid." And then—something cracked. The breath started to take over. Deeper. Faster. Continuous. My diaphragm trembled as if it had been asleep for decades and was finally waking up.

And then it hit—the tidal wave. Emotions I had buried so deep I didn't even have names for them began to rise. Rage. Grief. Shame. Guilt. My hands tingled. My arms went numb. My chest expanded so wide I thought it might split open. And then the sound came—a primal scream that had been living in my diaphragm for forty years ripped its way out of me. I cried like I had never cried before. I shook. I pounded the floor with my fists as if I could punch every unspoken word out of my body. And with every breath, something began to release, something old, something heavy, something I had carried for far too long.

Then came the vision. Out of nowhere, I saw the faces of the brothers I had lost in the Army—all gone to suicide. And in that moment, they were there with me. Standing around me in uniform. Not to haunt me, but to thank me. The message was clear and undeniable: *Thank you.* I felt it more than I heard it, vibrating through my bones, echoing through my breath. I knew, in a way words can't explain, that my healing was somehow theirs too. That the release happening through me was rippling through them across some unseen thread of consciousness.

I left that session undone. Changed. Something irreversible had happened. When I walked into the emergency room weeks before, I thought I was dying. When I walked out of that breath-work session, I knew I was being reborn.

That's how stark the contrast was. It wasn't subtle or poetic; it was a line in the sand. Before breath-work, I was a man drowning in my own silence. After breath-work, I was a man who had found air for the first time.

Since that day, breath-work has been my medicine. My ritual. My prayer. It became part of my morning routine and the foundation of my spiritual practice. It wasn't just about oxygen anymore—it was about energy. About vibration. About reclaiming the rhythm that trauma had stolen from me. Because here's what I've learned: every breath is a frequency. When you breathe shallow, your body hums in fear. When you breathe deeply and consciously, your entire system begins to resonate at a higher vibration—a vibration of safety, of presence, of life.

Breath-work taught me something the ER never could: I wasn't broken. I was holding too much. And the way back to myself wasn't through numbing or running—it was through breathing. Through feeling everything I had spent a lifetime avoiding.

And that was only the beginning.

Breath-work gave me what the ER never could: the realization that the very thing I had been doing unconsciously since birth—the one act that required no permission—was the gateway to everything I had been searching for. And the more I practiced, the more I understood: this wasn't new. It was ancient.

In yoga, they call it **prana**—life force. In Taoist practice, it's **qi,** the vital energy that animates all living things. In the Hebrew texts, the word **ruach** means both breath and spirit, as if to say they are inseparable. Indigenous traditions around the world have honored breath as the sacred thread between the physical and the unseen. Every culture that has survived the test of time has known this truth: breath is not just air moving through lungs—it is energy moving through existence.

And yet here we are, in the modern age, gasping under the weight of stress and technology, forgetting the very medicine built into our design. Science is finally catching up to what the sages knew: conscious breathing changes everything.

When you slow your breath, when you extend the exhale, you activate the **parasympathetic nervous system**, signaling safety to every cell. This isn't a metaphor—it's measurable. **Heart rate variability (HRV)** improves, and that's not just a number on a chart; it's an indicator of resilience, the body's ability to adapt to stress without collapsing. The **vagus nerve**, a wandering superhighway connecting your brain to your organs, lights up in response to slow, intentional breath, flooding the system with signals of calm. Cortisol—the hormone of fight or flight—drops. Dopamine and serotonin rebalance. In the span of a few breaths, the entire biochemistry of fear begins to shift toward peace.

And if you go deeper, something more profound begins to happen—something science is only beginning to map. Your **brain waves** slow from the frantic beta state of constant thinking into alpha and even theta, the frequencies of creativity, intuition, and healing. Your electromagnetic field, which the HeartMath Institute has studied extensively, begins to move into coherence—an elegant, harmonic rhythm where the heart and brain sync like instruments tuning to the same key. Breath, quite literally, raises your vibration.

This is why ancient traditions paired breath with prayer, movement, and meditation: because they understood that how you breathe determines how you live—and, on a subtle level, how you vibrate. Fear has a rhythm. So does peace. The question is: which one is pulsing through you right now?

But here's something few people consider: breathing patterns are inherited. Not genetically, but energetically and behaviorally. If your parents lived in fight-or-flight, you absorbed it before you ever had words. Babies mirror their caregivers' breath. If your mother held her breath when she was anxious, chances are you learned to do the same. If your father sighed in anger or paced in silence, your nervous system learned his rhythm. Breath becomes a family story—a generational frequency passed down like an heirloom.

And this is why conscious breathing is revolutionary. When you choose to breathe differently, you are not just regulating your own nervous system—you are disrupting patterns that may have lived in your bloodline for centuries. You are saying: *It ends with me.*

Every deep inhale is a reclamation. Every long exhale is a release of ghosts you didn't even know were haunting you. Breath-work isn't just self-care—it's lineage work.

I've seen this in my own life. With every breath-work session, I felt layers peeling away—not just my layers, but the ones I inherited. The silence of my father. The tension of my mother. The unspoken grief of generations shaped by survival. Breath became my scalpel and my salve, cutting through the scar tissue of time while soothing the wounds beneath.

And so I practice. Sometimes it's simple—eleven minutes of breath-work early in the morning. Sometimes it's intense—an hour of conscious connected breath that feels like diving into the underworld and resurfacing reborn. But every time, the principle remains the same: breath is the bridge. The bridge between chaos and calm. Between trauma and transcendence. Between who I've been and who I am becoming.

When I teach breath now, I don't teach it as a technique. I teach it as a return. A homecoming. Because at the core, breath reminds us of what we've forgotten: you are not your thoughts. You are not your emotions. You are not your body. You are not your history. You are the awareness breathing through all of it.

And that awareness is where we go next.

Thought: The Mind's Rhythm and the Return to Balance

Thought is the silent architect of your inner world. It organizes how you see yourself, how you see others, and how you see what's possible. Every decision, every reaction, every identity you've ever claimed has been constructed on the scaffolding of thought. And yet most of what passes through the mind isn't new—it's inherited. Conditioned. Recycled. Until you examine your thoughts with awareness, you're not thinking—you're echoing.

When I began breathwork, I started to feel again. The body that had been frozen for years began to thaw, and with it came sensations I didn't know how to name. But the next step was learning to think differently—to catch the subconscious loops that had been writing my life story without my consent. Breath opened the door, but my thoughts were the room I had to learn to move through without stumbling over the old furniture of my past.

This is where the principle of **homeostasis** enters the picture. In science, homeostasis refers to the body's ability to maintain internal stability—blood pressure, temperature, pH, and glucose levels. It's a balance. It's an order. It's the body saying, *We're okay here.* But what most people miss is this: homeostasis isn't just physical. It applies to our thoughts, our beliefs, and our emotional states, too.

If you've lived most of your life in chaos, fear, survival, and trauma, then chaos becomes your baseline. Your mind—like your body—will fight to return to what it knows. That is your mental homeostasis. For some, it means returning to anxiety after a few calm days because calm feels unsafe. For others, it's sabotaging success because struggle feels familiar. For many, it's seeking out relationships that mirror the dysfunction they grew up with, even when they swear they want something different. The mind is wired for what is known, not what is healthy.

And here lies the paradox: growth feels like danger. Transformation feels like a threat. Not because you're broken, but because your nervous system and thought patterns are designed to pull you back to what's familiar. The brain operates on **predictive coding**—it constantly forecasts the next moment based on the last million. When your past is soaked in trauma, your mind predicts more trauma, and your body responds accordingly. You're not anxious because something is wrong now—you're anxious because your system expects it.

Enter **hormesis**. Originally a biological concept, hormesis describes how small, controlled doses of stress—cold exposure, fasting, intense exercise—strengthen the body over time. It's the principle of resilience: temporary discomfort creates long-term adaptability. What most don't realize is that hormesis applies to the mind as well. Consciously confronting difficult thoughts, questioning old beliefs, and sitting in emotional discomfort can rewire your cognitive homeostasis.

When I first understood this, it changed everything. Because I realized that mental hormesis is the opposite of avoidance. It's leaning into the discomfort of awareness instead of running from it. It's asking the hard questions:

- Is this thought helping me regulate or dysregulate?
- Is this thought rooted in love or in fear?
- Is this thought even mine, or did I inherit it from someone else's pain?

These questions became my internal compass. They helped me see that most of what I called "me" was just an echo of generations. I carried my father's skepticism, my mother's worry, my culture's obsession with control—all running like background programs shaping my reality. And this is where thought meets energy.

Because thought isn't just abstract, it's electrical. Every time you think, neurons fire, and those firings create electromagnetic fields measurable outside your skull. Your brain hums at frequencies—from frantic beta when you're stressed, to calm alpha when you're focused, to dreamy theta when you slip into deep meditation. These aren't just states—they are vibrations, and they dictate what you perceive as real. The more your thoughts loop in fear, the more your brain locks into beta waves, the frequency of hypervigilance. The more you choose thoughts of safety, gratitude, or possibility, the more you shift toward coherence—your heart and brain syncing like instruments tuning to the same note.

And so the question became: what frequency am I broadcasting to myself? Because thoughts are not private whispers—they are instructions to your nervous system. Every fear-based thought sends a chemical signal, flooding the body with cortisol, adrenaline, and tension. Every loving thought sends a different one—releasing oxytocin, serotonin, and calm. Thought is chemistry in motion. Thought is vibration in form.

This is why transformation feels like chaos before it feels like peace: because you're not just changing habits—you're dismantling the electrical grid your identity has been running on for decades. Your brain will resist because the unfamiliar feels unsafe. Your old self will fight for survival. But every time you breathe through a fear instead of reacting, every time you choose a conscious thought over an unconscious loop, you're creating a new rhythm. You're teaching your mind a new frequency.

And that's what this section is really about: learning the rhythm of thought the way you learned the rhythm of breath. Because when the mind spins unchecked, when its loops are tangled with inherited pain, it becomes an echo chamber of survival. But when you slow down and listen—not to obey, but to observe—you begin to reclaim authorship. You start to write your own narrative instead of recycling someone else's.

***** So let's pause again. This time, close your eyes, take a deep breath, hold for 5 seconds (5, 4, 3, 2, & 1), and exhale for a long 10 seconds (10, 9, 8, 7, 6, 5, 4, 3, 2, & 1). Keep your eyes close for 60 seconds and count down. Then open your eyes and feel*****

So I ask you—how did you feel during the meditation? How do you feel now? What you accomplished in one minute was the separation of your thoughts and emotions by interrupting the nervous system through a deep breath and focusing the mind on a 60-second countdown. In this minute, you gain control of yourself, you become present, and three things happen. You activated the body, interrupted the mind, and when the meditation was over, you felt your awareness. Good job.

Inherited Loops and the Weight of Generations

Most of us assume our thoughts are ours. We believe the voice in our head belongs to us, that every opinion, every judgment, every fear is original. But pause long enough and you'll notice: much of what you think is hand-me-down language. You didn't choose it—you absorbed it.

Your parents gave you more than DNA. They gave you patterns—ways of seeing, scripts for reacting, frameworks for what's possible and what isn't. Some of these were spoken outright: "Don't trust people," "Life is hard," "Money doesn't grow on trees." Others were unspoken, coded into the sigh after a long day, the tension in a jawline, the silence that filled a room like fog. Children are sponges, and what they soak in becomes the water they swim in for life.

And this isn't just psychology—it's energy. Every thought is an electrical impulse traveling neural highways, but thoughts don't stop there. They radiate. They become fields. They ripple through families, through generations, until someone notices the tide. Neuroscience calls this epigenetics—how trauma and stress in one generation leave molecular imprints that influence the next. Spiritually, we've always known it as generational patterns, karmic loops, and ancestral memory. Different languages for the same truth: what isn't healed is handed down.

When you grow up in an environment where fear hums like background music, your nervous system tunes to that frequency. It becomes normal. It becomes homeostasis. And then decades later, you wonder why calm feels foreign, why joy feels suspicious, why love feels like a risk. You're not broken—you're programmed. You inherited the survival code of your bloodline, and that code speaks through thought.

I saw this clearly during my own awakening. After breath-work cracked me open, after the tears and tremors and visions, I started to watch my mind like a hawk. And what I found was sobering: most of what I believed about myself was never mine. The shame, the scarcity, the relentless pressure to perform—it wasn't my voice. It was my father's silence disguised as self-doubt. It was my mother's anxiety dressed up as caution. It was the collective hum of a family that had survived more storms than stories could hold, and now those storms were raging in me.

I remember one morning in particular. I was journaling after a breath session, feeling raw and exposed, and I wrote: *Whose voice is this?* That question changed everything. Because when you ask it with honesty, you begin to see the architecture of your identity—and you realize most of the bricks aren't yours.

And here's the thing: awareness of the pattern doesn't erase it. The loops still come. The old thoughts still surface like ghosts, whispering the same tired lines: *You're not enough. You'll fail. It's safer to stay small.* But when you know the voice isn't yours, you don't have to obey it. You can choose. And choice is the beginning of liberation.

This is where energy and frequency become more than concepts. Thoughts carry charge. They are measurable in the brain as micro-currents, but they are also felt—viscerally. Fear vibrates fast and shallow, like jittery static. Love vibrates wide and slow, like a deep ocean swell. Every thought you entertain is a tuning fork for your nervous system. When you loop fear-based thoughts long enough, your body hums in dissonance. Your heart rate spikes. Cortisol floods your blood. The immune system falters. Not because life is attacking you—but because your internal symphony is out of tune.

And the opposite is true. When you begin to shift your mental frequency—even slightly—the whole system responds. Gratitude isn't just a nice idea; it's neurochemical. Thoughts of appreciation trigger dopamine and oxytocin, rewiring your brain toward connection and safety. Over time, repetition becomes reality. This is neuroplasticity—the brain's ability to remodel itself based on what you think, feel, and do. And this is why conscious thought is not just self-help fluff—it's a survival strategy. It's energy hygiene.

But here's the challenge: you can't think your way out of trauma with the same mind that trauma built. You can't just sprinkle affirmations on an unhealed wound and call it wholeness. That's why breath came first for me. Breath calmed the body so the mind could open. Breath lowered the static so new signals could get through. And once I could breathe, I could begin to choose.

And that's when the real work started. Because thought isn't just about affirmations—it's about attention where you place it, what you feed. And for someone who lived decades in survival mode, attention was a battlefield. My mind wanted to scan for threats, to predict disaster, to rehearse failure. It wasn't trying to hurt me—it was trying to protect me. That's what minds do. But the protection became a prison, and the bars were made of thought.

Breaking those bars required practice. Moment by moment. Breath by breath. Asking every day: *What frequency am I tuning to right now?* Fear or love? Scarcity or abundance? Echo or truth? And every time I caught the echo, every time I chose a different note, I felt the vibration shift. Slowly, subtly, but undeniably.

The Practice and the Shift

Once I understood that thought wasn't the truth, that it was simply patterned electricity firing through well-worn circuits, the question became: *How do I change the pattern?* And the answer wasn't to force new thoughts in through sheer willpower. I had tried that before—positive thinking, affirmations—but nothing stuck, because the ground beneath the thoughts was still unstable.

What I needed was awareness paired with repetition, but not the kind of robotic repetition that ignores the body's reality. I needed rhythm. I needed the mind to learn what the breath had already begun to teach the body: safety.

So I started treating my thoughts like vital signs. Every morning, I would check in the way a nurse checks a pulse. I would notice the first thoughts that surfaced before I even got out of bed. Sometimes they were quiet but corrosive: *You're already behind. Today's going to be hard.* Other times they were loud, almost panicked: *What if it all falls apart?* These weren't random. They were echoes of yesterday and the day before, carrying the residue of a nervous system still wired for threat.

Instead of wrestling with them, I began observing them. Naming them. Breathing through them. And then gently replacing them—not with grandiose affirmations that felt fake, but with thoughts that felt possible: *I am here. I am safe in this moment. One breath at a time.* Over time, those small shifts compounded. New neural pathways started to form, and with them came new sensations in the body. What once felt like chaos started to feel like coherence.

Science backs this up. Every thought strengthens the network it fires through, a principle known as Hebbian learning: "Neurons that fire together wire together." When you think the same thought repeatedly, you reinforce that circuitry until it becomes automatic. But the inverse is also true: when you interrupt the old pattern and choose a new one, you weaken the old wiring and strengthen the new. This is **neuroplasticity**. It is the brain's ability to rewire itself in response to experience.

And experience isn't just mental—it's energetic. Every time you shift a thought from fear to safety, from shame to self-acceptance, you're not just creating new synapses—you're shifting your frequency. Your brain waves respond. Instead of the jagged, rapid spikes of beta—the signature of stress—you begin to experience more alpha, the smooth waves of focus and calm. Sometimes, even theta, the deep, fluid rhythm of intuition and healing. In these states, the heart and brain synchronize, creating what researchers call **coherence**. And coherence isn't just a scientific term—it's a felt sense. It's the quiet hum inside you when everything stops clashing and starts harmonizing.

For me, that hum became the signal. When my thoughts pulled me into spirals of fear, I felt the dissonance in my chest. When I shifted toward presence, I felt the soft tuning of harmony. Over time, I realized this wasn't just mental hygiene—it was energy work. Because thoughts don't stay in the brain; they echo through the entire field of your being. They shape the way your cells express, the way your nervous system fires, the way your life unfolds.

But here's the paradox: the goal isn't to stop thinking. It's not to wage war on the mind. That only adds more noise. The goal is to see thought for what it is—movement. Activity. Like waves on the surface of the ocean. When you're fused with them, you feel every crash as a catastrophe. When you step back and watch, you realize they're just waves. Rising. Falling. Dissolving.

And this is where the work of thought begins to blur into the realm of something greater—the realm of awareness. Because no matter how refined your thoughts become, no matter how positive or elevated or intentional, if you're still identified with them, you're still in the cage. A prettier cage, maybe, but a cage nonetheless. ***True freedom isn't thinking better thoughts—it's knowing you are not your thoughts at all.***

This is where we go next. Into the silence beneath the noise. Into the witness behind the narrative. Into the space that was there before the first thought ever appeared—the space that has been waiting, patiently, for you to notice.

Awareness: The Silence That Sees All

Awareness doesn't shout. It doesn't compete. It doesn't argue. It waits—patiently—beneath the chaos of your thoughts, the storm of your emotions, and the storylines of your trauma. It is the quiet witness that has been there from the beginning, untouched by the dramas you call your life, unshaken by the tides of joy or despair.

But in a world addicted to noise—notifications, headlines, endless scrolls, mental chatter—we forget this witness exists. We live in our minds the way fish live in water, blind to the fact that we are submerged in something we didn't choose and can't see. We mistake the current for the ocean. We mistake the wave for the self. And so we spend our days tossed from one thought to the next, one emotion to the next, believing this turbulence is who we are.

But it's not.

Awareness is the space between breaths. The gap between the end of an exhale and the rise of the next inhale. It's that pause you rarely notice—the doorway you rarely walk through. Awareness is not thought. It is what sees thought. It is the silence behind the voice in your head, the stillness behind the heartbeat, the presence that has watched every identity you've worn and never once confused itself with any of them. It was the observer hearing the drum of your heartbeat when you counted down from 60 in the last exercise.

The doorway to this awareness is silence. But silence terrifies us. Why? Because silence exposes what noise hides. In silence, you can hear the things you've been running from: the echo of grief you never named, the hum of fear beneath your achievements, the truth that all your doing has never brought you home. This is why we fill every spare second with sound—with music, with conversations, with podcasts, with the white noise of busyness—because silence feels like a mirror, and most of us are afraid to look.

When I first sat in that silence, it was brutal. After breath-work cracked me open, after the flood of emotions and visions and the first taste of what freedom might feel like, I thought meditation would be easy. It wasn't. It felt like being trapped in the heart of a hurricane, with nothing solid to cling to. My mind screamed. My body twitched. My thoughts did cartwheels, inventing reasons to quit: *You're wasting time. This isn't working. You should be doing something productive.* Every part of me wanted to escape. And yet, something deeper—something older—knew this was the work.

So I stayed. Ten minutes at first. Then twenty. Sometimes crying. Sometimes bargaining with the clock. Always returning to the breath. Always returning to the body. Until one day, something shifted. The thoughts didn't disappear—they kept moving, like clouds across the sky—but I stopped chasing them. I stopped trying to make them go away. I stopped trying to fix or manage, or curate what was happening in my head. And in that surrender, something else appeared.

Silence. Not the kind you hear with your ears, but the kind you feel. A silence that wasn't empty but full—full of everything I had been avoiding. And yet, instead of crushing me, it held me. It was as if I had fallen backward into a vast space that had always been there, waiting, patient as stone. And for the first time in my life, I wasn't trying to control anything. I wasn't running or hiding or performing. I was simply aware.

And here's what that awareness revealed: that the self I had been defending all those years—the anxious achiever, the man chasing validation, the soldier braced for attack—wasn't me. It was a costume stitched together from thoughts and experiences, from wounds and roles and borrowed voices. Underneath all of that was something wordless. Something still. Something unbreakable.

Science has a name for what happens when you touch this space: the **default mode network** (DMN)—the part of the brain responsible for self-referential thinking—quiets down. This is the network that spins the story of "me": my past, my future, my plans, my failures. It's useful for survival, but exhausting when it never shuts off. Meditation softens its grip. Over time, consistent practice reduces DMN activity, increases gray matter in the prefrontal cortex, and strengthens emotional regulation. Cortisol drops. Blood pressure lowers. In other words: stillness heals.

But beyond the science, awareness does something no metric can measure: it rewires your relationship with reality. Because when you sit long enough in silence, you begin to see that life isn't happening to you or even for you—it's happening through you. You are not the storm, you are the sky. And once you know that, nothing outside you can shake the ground inside you.

This doesn't mean life becomes easy. The storms still come. The thoughts still chatter. The body still aches. But awareness gives you something nothing else can: the ability to stand in the middle of chaos without becoming it. To feel the rise of anger without punching walls. To feel the pull of fear without collapsing. To hold grief like a stone in your hand without drowning in it. Awareness is the space where choice is born. And choice, when it comes from awareness, is freedom.

The Field Beyond Thought

The deeper I sank into awareness, the more I realized something radical: awareness isn't inside you—everything else is inside it. The body, the mind, the thoughts you mistake for self, even the pain you swear defines you—all of it floats in awareness like clouds in an endless sky. And the sky doesn't cling to clouds. It doesn't resist storms or chase sunsets. It just is. Limitless. Untouched. Watching.

When I first glimpsed this, it was disorienting. For decades, I thought of consciousness as something my brain produced, like a signal flickering inside my skull. But in the stillness, that illusion collapsed. Awareness wasn't trapped in my head. It wasn't local at all. It felt boundless—as if my breath and the space around me were made of the same substance, as if the edges of "me" had dissolved into something vast and benevolent.

Mystics have spoken of this for centuries. The Upanishads call it **Atman**—the self beyond self. Taoism calls it the **Tao**—the unnameable source flowing through all things. Science, though still catching up, points to a similar wonder: what if consciousness isn't an accident of neurons but the fundamental field from which everything emerges? Theories like **Integrated Information** and **Panpsychism** suggest that awareness might not be a byproduct of matter—it might be the ground of reality itself.

Why does this matter for healing? Because the moment you identify with the space instead of the storm, the entire relationship with pain changes.

Trauma loses its teeth. Anxiety loses its throne. You still feel it—you're human—but you're no longer fused with it. The emotion surges, but you don't drown. The thought screams, but you don't obey. Because awareness doesn't cling. Awareness allows. And what is allowed begins to move.

This is how generational trauma dissolves—not by erasing history but by no longer feeding the loop. Every pattern, every echo of survival, thrives on unconsciousness. It needs you to believe the thought, to obey the fear, to mistake the voice for truth. Awareness serves that contract. It doesn't fight the loop; it watches it. And in the watching, the loop unravels. Not overnight, but steadily. Like a knot loosening in warm water.

I saw this in my own practice. There were days when old narratives rose like ghosts: *You're failing. You're unsafe. You'll end up alone.* Before, those words would have swallowed me. They would have dictated my choices, my mood, my entire day. But in awareness, something different happened. The voice came—and I saw it. Noticed its texture, its tone, its pull. And instead of reacting, I breathed. I let it pass like weather across an open sky. And every time I did, the voice lost power. The identification thinned. The knot loosened.

From an energetic lens, this makes perfect sense—thoughts are vibrations, emotions are vibrations, and trauma is simply condensed vibration, a high-intensity signal trapped within the nervous system, looping endlessly because the mind continues to energize it with attention and resistance. But awareness changes the equation; when you stop resisting and begin witnessing, the frequency begins to shift. What was once dense and immovable slowly starts to disperse, and in its place, coherence begins to replace chaos. This is not just poetic language—it is physiological truth. The vagus nerve begins to calm, heart rate variability stabilizes, and brain waves soften, moving from beta to alpha and into the deeper states of theta. Stillness becomes medicine—not because of some mystical force, but because it restores harmony at every level: cellular, neural, and energetic.

But awareness is not only healing—it is deeply liberating. Because in the quiet that follows, a truth begins to emerge, a truth no book, no teacher, and no doctrine could ever fully give you: that you are not the body, not the mind, and not even the sum of your life's experiences—you are the presence that is aware of them all. And that presence is untouchable. It existed long before the first wound ever formed and will remain long after the final scar has faded.

I remember the first time this truth landed in me—not as a concept or idea, but as a direct and undeniable experience. I was sitting on the floor, my back resting against the wall, eyes gently closed. My body ached from days of somatic release, and my mind was exhausted from its own relentless noise. And then—silence. Not the kind of silence that comes from a quiet room, but a deeper, internal silence. A pause so vast it felt infinite. In that pause, everything fell away: the story of who I believed I was, the weight of all I had done, and the fear of what might come—gone. What remained was something so simple, so clear it felt eternal: awareness aware of itself. Nothing missing. Nothing broken.

Tears fell, not from sadness, but from the deep relief of finally letting go. Because in that moment, I finally understood what I had been searching for all along: home. Not a home built from walls, roles, or relationships, but a home that could never be taken away and never be lost—a home that had always been here, quietly waiting for me to notice it.

And this is the paradox that changes everything: the healing you've been chasing isn't something you have to earn—it's something you simply uncover. It has been here all along, buried beneath the noise and the narrative, waiting for the courage to become still.

Life in the Space Between

When awareness stops being an idea and becomes a living reality, everything changes—not because the world softens its edges, but because you stop cutting yourself on them. The emails still come. The deadlines still press. People still act out their pain in ways that once hooked you like barbed wire. But in awareness, there's space—space between stimulus and response, between the trigger and the choice. And in that space, freedom is born.

I used to live without that space. I was all reaction—wired to defend, to explain, to fight or flee. Every sharp word was a threat. Every challenge was a verdict on my worth. Awareness didn't erase the sharpness of life; it simply revealed that the blade was never aimed at who I really am. It showed me that what gets cut is the costume, not the core.

This is the practical gift of awareness: emotional regulation at its deepest level. Not forced calm. Not spiritual bypassing. Real regulation—the kind that doesn't come from controlling life but from no longer being controlled by it. When fear rises, you feel it, but you don't fuse with it. When anger sparks, you see it before it burns down the house. When grief knocks, you open the door without collapsing in its arms. Awareness turns every emotion into a weather passing through the sky of your being.

Science confirms what mystics have lived for millennia: consistent meditation reshapes the brain. Studies on long-term practitioners show increased **gamma wave activity**—associated with heightened awareness and compassion—along with thicker gray matter in regions linked to memory, empathy, and decision-making. The **amygdala**, that tiny almond-shaped alarm bell, shrinks in size, while the prefrontal cortex strengthens. In other words: awareness doesn't just make you feel different—it rewires who you are.

And yet, the most profound shift can't be measured on an fMRI. It's vibrational. When you live as awareness, your frequency changes. Coherence becomes your baseline. The jagged edges of survival soften into the smooth hum of presence. People feel it. Animals feel it. Rooms shift when you walk in—not because you're performing peace, but because you've become a tuning fork for it. This is what ancient traditions meant by alignment—not a posture but a resonance. When your inner field stabilizes, chaos outside loses its grip.

This matters because life won't stop being life. The storms will come. The losses will sting. The unexpected will arrive at inconvenient hours. Awareness doesn't spare you the human experience—it saturates it. You taste it fully because you're no longer numbed by avoidance or hijacked by reactivity. You cry without drowning. You love without clinging. You succeed without selling your soul. And when pain comes—and it will—you hold it like a stone in the palm of your hand, feeling its weight without becoming its gravity.

For me, this shift unfolded quietly. There was no fireworks moment, no halo of enlightenment. Just subtle changes, like threads pulling loose from an old fabric. I stopped snapping at the people I loved. I stopped believing every story my mind told me. I stopped chasing every high and fearing every low. And in that stillness, something extraordinary emerged—not an escape from life, but a deeper intimacy with it.

Because here's the secret: awareness doesn't remove you from the world—it roots you in it more fully than ever. You notice the way light pools on a wooden floor. You hear the hum of your own breath as if for the first time. You taste water like it's a miracle. When you're no longer lost in the mind's movie, the raw, unscripted beauty of life floods in. This is the gift that breath and thought were pointing toward all along: not control, not perfection, but presence.

And that brings us to the truth at the heart of this chapter: healing isn't a destination. It's not a mountain you climb to plant a flag at the summit. Healing is this—this breath, this thought observed instead of obeyed, this silence deep enough to hold both without needing to fix either. Healing is awareness remembering itself in the middle of the mess.

Breath was the doorway—the rhythm that pulled me out of chaos and back into the body. Thought was the next frontier—the terrain of loops and echoes where I learned to choose instead of react. And awareness was the ground beneath them all—the unshakable space where healing happens not through doing but through being.

This is the arc. Breathing regulates the nervous system. Thought rewires the mind. Awareness liberates the self from the illusion of both. And when these three move together—when breath slows, thought softens, and awareness expands—you enter a state no storm can shatter: coherence. Harmony. Wholeness.

Not because life got easier, but because you remembered the truth that was here before the wound, before the fear, before the first inhale you ever took: you are not the waves—you are the ocean.

And the ocean never breaks.

Chapter Nine
Transformation - The Ongoing Becoming

> **"In the middle of difficulty lies opportunity."**
>
> — *Albert Einstein*

After enduring six months of relentless panic attacks and two years of unraveling and integrating four decades of unprocessed pain, I thought transformation would eventually feel like a completed work, something whole and permanent, as if life would one day deliver me to a finish line where peace stood waiting like an old friend. But what I discovered—and what I resisted for far too long—is that transformation does not conclude; it evolves, it spirals, it dissolves the illusion of arrival and invites us into something far more humbling: the recognition that there is no ultimate destination because becoming is a process without borders.

The mind—our faithful architect of stories—clings to the notion of completion. It whispers that if we work hard enough, heal deep enough, and forgive thoroughly enough, then the past will no longer shadow us and we will finally inhabit a life free from fracture. But this belief belongs to a consciousness bound to time, to beginnings and endings, to the seductive idea of a straight path rather than the truth of an infinite, circular unfolding. In reality, life is movement—energy perpetually in motion, forming and reforming, breaking and mending, ebbing and surging like water against stone. We are not static structures; we are rivers carving through the landscapes of experience, and even when the water's still, there is motion beneath the surface.

For years, I lived under the illusion that permanence was something to be secured, by striving harder, by shaping an identity, by erecting roles sturdy enough to withstand the erosion of time. When I finally embraced teaching, guiding immigrants through the labyrinth of a new language and culture, I believed

I had arrived at a vocation that could carry me through the rest of my life. I loved that work. It was meaningful, connective, deeply human. For the first time in years, I felt anchored. And yet, life—ever committed to our evolution—does not allow anchors for long. Two weeks before writing these words, that chapter closed with a single conversation, a polite but irrevocable notice that my role was ending. And though logic offered alternatives—return to school, secure the credential, rebuild the scaffolding—I felt, beneath the noise, the same truth that met me during my deepest descent: endings are not failures. They are invitations.

Had that door not closed, this book—the one I have known in my bones needed to exist—might have lingered in the margins for years. Instead, I found myself waking each day to the blank page, no longer running, no longer bargaining for permanence, but listening for what life was asking of me now. And in that listening, I returned to a truth I had touched before but never fully allowed: transformation is not a single rupture or a sudden rebirth; it is the quiet rhythm between what is dissolving and what is emerging, the space where the old self has lost its grip and the new self has not yet taken form.

This space is not comfortable. It feels like groundlessness, like walking across an invisible bridge that reveals itself only underfoot. But it is here—in the liminal, in the in-between—that consciousness learns to breathe outside the armor of identity. Transformation, I now understand, is not the dramatic clash between death and rebirth but the subtle awareness that both are occurring at once, continuously, within and around us.

And so I began to write—not because I had resolved everything, but because I had surrendered to the truth that nothing stays resolved. That life, in its essence, is a series of dissolutions and integrations. That the self I grieved yesterday becomes the soil for the self I will embody tomorrow. And that somewhere beyond all of it—the rise and the fall, the rupture and repair—there is something untouched, something that watches without fear, something that is not becoming because it has always been.

Recovery as Ritual: The Architecture of Healing

Recovery, I've learned, does not arrive unannounced like a gift dropped at your doorstep; it is something you choose, deliberately and often imperfectly, every single day. For a long time, I thought healing would happen in one sweeping moment—a cathartic release, a single transcendent experience that would dissolve years of suffering. But true recovery is not an event. It is an architecture, a structure built through rhythm and devotion, through small, sacred choices repeated until they become a language the body recognizes as safety.

After the collapse—the panic attacks, the nights spent bargaining with breath, the weeks where silence felt unbearable—I began to understand that survival had been my only operating system for decades. My nervous system, shaped by war, dysfunction, and inherited scarcity, had learned to live in vigilance. Even in stillness, I was bracing. Even in joy, I was scanning for a threat. And so recovery could not be passive. It required conscious interruption of patterns that had calcified across generations, patterns that whispered work harder, move faster, prove more, because safety is conditional and rest is dangerous.

This is why my mornings became sacred ground. Before the noise of the world could reclaim me, I claimed myself. I woke before dawn—not because discipline is virtuous, but because presence is fragile and must be invited before the day can erode it. I made sleep non-negotiable, not out of indulgence but necessity, because the science is unambiguous: without at least seven hours of quality rest, the body cannot repair cellular damage, cannot regulate hormones, cannot quiet the amygdala's alarm. Chronic sleep deprivation is not a badge of productivity; it is a slow erosion of every system that sustains life.

So I began where life begins—with water. A full glass before words, before screens, before thought itself. Hydration is not trivial. It is the medium through which electrical signals travel, the current that keeps neurons firing, muscles contracting, organs humming. To drink water in the morning is to remind the body that you are supported, you are alive, and you are more than machinery running on habit.

Then I moved—not violently, not in the punishing cadence of old gym rituals, but intuitively, in dialogue with my own tissues. Ten minutes of yoga, breath tethered to motion, fascia slowly unfurling like roots in soft soil. Trauma, science now confirms, does not reside only in memory; it lives in muscle fibers, in the viscera, in the rigid scaffolding we mistake for posture. Gentle movement is not aesthetic; it is liberation, a somatic invitation for stored stories to loosen their grip.

After movement came breath—twelve minutes of deliberate, conscious breathing, sometimes soft and circular, sometimes sharp and rhythmic, always anchored in the recognition that breath is the hinge between body and awareness. Breath-work is not esoteric; it is physiological medicine. With each inhale, the vagus nerve whispers safety to the heart. With each exhale, the sympathetic storm recedes. This is not a metaphor; it is measurable. Heart rate variability improves. Cortisol declines. The brain shifts from survival's narrow tunnel to the panoramic vista of regulation.

And then, silence. Meditation is not a strategy to escape thought but a return to the witness that observes thought without drowning in it. Some days ten minutes. Some days forty-five. Not seeking enlightenment, not seeking anything at all, but remembering the simple miracle of being aware. In those moments, the mind—so frantic in its rehearsals and regrets—softened. Not disappeared, but softened, like a tide receding enough for the sand to appear beneath.

When possible, I closed the ritual with cold—a plunge into water salted with ice, the body's instinctive panic rising like a siren and then quieting as breath reclaimed the throne. This practice, which some dismiss as spectacle, is an ancient dialogue between organism and environment, a conversation that rewires resilience. Cold exposure stimulates brown fat activation, sharpens mitochondrial efficiency, and floods the system with norepinephrine—a chemical hymn to wakefulness and repair. But beyond the biochemistry, cold teaches presence. You cannot dissociate in freezing water. You must inhabit the body fully, or you will suffer. And in that full inhabitation, fear loses its empire.

This, for me, is recovery. Not a checklist. Not a performative routine. But a series of thresholds—water, breath, stillness, cold—through which I return, again and again, to the truth that peace is not found. It is cultivated, and that cultivation begins not in the grand gestures but in the quiet, repetitive motions that tell the nervous system: you are safe now. You can rest.

The Moment of Singularity: When Energy and Awareness Converge

There comes a point in every transformation when the past refuses to remain buried, when the body—after years of silent endurance—calls a reckoning that cannot be negotiated away. For me, that moment arrived without warning on an ordinary day, behind the wheel of my car, on a stretch of freeway I had driven a hundred times before. One second, I was immersed in the rhythm of traffic, and the next, I was drowning in a tide of symptoms so violent they eclipsed thought itself. Breath vanished. Limbs turned to stone. Vision narrowed. My heart became a drum of war inside my chest, and a voice I could not quiet screamed the words we all fear most: *You are dying.*

I pulled over, clinging to the steering wheel as if it could tether me to existence, and in that suffocating interval between inhale and exhale, I believed with absolute certainty that this was my ending. No abstract fear, no hypothetical scenario—this was visceral, primal, undeniable. What I did not know then, what no one had taught me to recognize, was that this was not death approaching but the body's last, desperate attempt to survive itself. It was not a heart attack, not some catastrophic failure of tissue or vessel. It was a severe panic attack—though such words feel inadequate for an event that detonates every circuit of being.

The emergency room confirmed what my body could not believe: blood pressure stable, oxygen normal, EKG clear. I was not dying, at least not in the way I thought. But something had indeed ruptured—not in my arteries, but in the architecture of self I had spent decades constructing. That day was not an outlier; it was the opening of a door I had prayed would stay shut. Over the next six months, panic became my shadow, stalking me through the most mundane moments, seizing me with electric fire that raced through nerves and marrow. Dizziness. Chest constriction. Numbness in my hands. The terror of my own biology.

Science offers a framework for what happened: a nervous system imprisoned in sympathetic overdrive, the hypothalamic-pituitary-adrenal axis flooding my bloodstream with cortisol, catecholamines turning my inner terrain into a battlefield. However, such terms cannot capture the existential unraveling, the way reality itself seemed to collapse inward like a dying star. This was more than physiology; it was a reckoning with forty years of stored sorrow, anger, shame—a lifetime of unresolved signals encoded not only in neurons but in fascia, in the very cadence of my breath.

And yet, this collapse—this implosion of all I thought I was—became the portal. The body that had carried me through war, through heartbreak, through the quiet violence of self-abandonment, had finally rebelled against the tyranny of suppression. What I had refused to feel, it now demanded I face. What I had numbed with work, drowned with noise, buried beneath performance—it dragged to the surface, raw and unrelenting. I could not run, because the battlefield was inside me. I could not fight, because the enemy was not real—it was memory, sensation, chemistry, and energy tangled in loops too ancient to untie with logic.

Here, in the ashes of control, I encountered something I had never known: *awareness*. Not as a concept, not as a spiritual ideal, but as a living presence that arrived when everything else failed. In the midst of panic, when the mind's machinery sputtered and the body convulsed under the weight of its own alarms, there emerged a quiet observer—a stillness that did not resist the storm but bore witness to it. And in that witnessing, something shifted. Not all at once. Not as liberation, but as a subtle recognition that I was not what was unraveling. I was the space in which the unraveling occurred.

This was my singularity—not a grand epiphany, but a convergence of biology, memory, and consciousness collapsing into a single point of undeniable truth: I could no longer live as a fragment of myself. Integration was no longer optional. It was the only way forward.

Understanding Energy: The Language of Life

To understand what happened to me, I had to abandon the shallow language of symptom and diagnosis and dive into the elemental fabric of existence. Everything, I came to realize—not as a philosophical cliché but as an embodied certainty—is energy. This is not a metaphor; it is physics. Strip matter to its smallest particles, and you find vibration, frequency, oscillation—patterns of movement woven into the lattice of reality. The body is not an exception; it is an expression. Your breath, your pulse, your thoughts, your grief—all are configurations of energy in motion or energy bound in stillness.

Science names these states with clinical precision: kinetic energy, the current of movement; potential energy, the silent reservoir waiting to be stirred; thermal energy, the warmth of molecular friction; electrical energy, the charge that animates neurons and muscles. But beneath the jargon lies a truth that reshaped my entire understanding of healing: the stories we suppress, the tears we swallow, the rage we chain in the basement of our being—these are not abstractions. They are energy rendered dense, coiled like serpents in muscle and fascia, humming at frequencies so low they pull the body into gravity's shadow.

When panic ravaged me, it was not random chaos; it was the body's attempt to discharge decades of potential energy that had been imprisoned by shame, fear, and generational silence. My trembling during breath-work, the convulsions that felt like an exorcism—these were not pathological. They were alchemical. Potential became kinetic. Stagnation dissolved into flow. And in that flow, something deeper occurred: vibration shifted. Frequency lifted.

This is why healing is not solely psychological. It is vibrational, electromagnetic, and somatic. Each breath, each sob, each primal tremor is a recalibration, a re-tuning of the instrument we inhabit. The ancients intuited this long before EEGs mapped brainwaves or fMRI scans lit up neural pathways. Yogis spoke of prana. Shamans of life force. Mystics of the divine pulse that threads through flesh and star alike. Today, we dress these truths in the garments of science, but their essence remains unchanged: to live is to oscillate, to vibrate in resonance with the great rhythm of existence. And when trauma distorts that rhythm, when inherited fear drags our frequency into discord, the work is not to escape the body but to liberate the music trapped within it.

Vibration and Frequency: The Invisible Architecture

The more I surrendered to the process of healing, the more I began to feel what language could not easily contain—that everything I experienced, from terror to serenity, was not merely emotional or mental but vibrational. Energy does not remain static; it hums, oscillates, and pulses at specific speeds that we call frequency. This is not esoteric conjecture—it is measurable, observable, the language of both physics and biology. Every atom vibrates. Every cell emits an electromagnetic field. The human heart generates a measurable rhythm, broadcasting frequencies that can be detected several feet beyond the body. Thought itself is an electrical event, and emotion, once felt, becomes a biochemical symphony, altering the amplitude of that signal.

When I was locked in panic, my vibration was jagged, my frequency low and chaotic, like static devouring the signal of a song. Fear constricts. It contracts the breath, tightens the fascia, accelerates the pulse until the body becomes an echo chamber for survival's siren. And when this state persists—not for moments but for years—it reshapes the architecture of being. Neural pathways harden around threat perception. Cortisol becomes a constant tide, corroding the shorelines of health. This is not simply stress. It is an entrainment to the frequency of danger, a resonance with scarcity, with vigilance, often inherited across bloodlines as epigenetic whispers telling the body: the world is not safe.

Science calls this allostatic load—the cumulative burden of chronic stress imprinted on systems designed for short bursts of emergency, not lifelong siege. But beyond the metrics of blood pressure and inflammation, there is a subtler truth: prolonged resonance with fear drags the entire vibrational signature downward. It thickens the field and densifies the energy until joy feels inaccessible, not because it is absent but because the bandwidth of perception has narrowed.

Conversely, when we begin to breathe deeply, to move gently, to speak the unspoken, something extraordinary unfolds: the waveform changes. Gratitude, love, awe—these states are not poetic indulgences; they are frequencies, measurable in hertz, observable in coherence between heart and brain. Research from the HeartMath Institute reveals that emotions like appreciation generate a harmonic rhythm in the heart's electromagnetic field, a pattern that ripples through the nervous system and radiates beyond the body. In such states, the organism moves from chaos to order, from fragmentation to flow.

This is why ancient practices—chanting, prayer, breath control, ritual movement—have endured across millennia. Long before EEGs traced gamma oscillations or HRV monitors graphed coherence, our ancestors understood that sound, stillness, and rhythm could recalibrate the hidden architecture of being. Trauma, too, is rhythmic—an internal dissonance sustained by silence and repetition. To heal is to alter the tempo, to reintroduce harmony where distortion ruled.

Generational trauma complicates this work. Patterns of fear and scarcity are not only transmitted through stories or parenting styles; they are etched into gene expression, shaping hormonal baselines, stress responses, and even the density of gray matter in regions linked to vigilance. The child of war carries the war in their cells. The granddaughter of famine feels hunger in ways that defy logic. These inherited frequencies hum beneath awareness until interrupted—through breath, through movement, through the radical act of presence. When I began to re-pattern my mornings, when I plunged into cold water, when I chose stillness over speed, I was not only tending to my own nervous system. I was breaking a frequency chain forged by centuries of survival.

And so, vibration became my compass. Not as an abstract metric, but as a felt sense, a resonance that told me whether I was contracting toward fear or expanding toward trust. In this way, healing ceased to be a linear march toward an endpoint and became what it truly is: an attunement, a return to a song older than language, a melody the body remembers even when the mind forgets.

The Trilogy of Becoming: Transmutation, Transcendence, & Transformation

If recovery was the architecture and awareness the foundation, then the pillars upon which my becoming rested were threefold: transmutation, transcendence, transformation. These words, often diluted by overuse, became for me not slogans but living processes, each distinct yet inseparable, each arising when the body, the mind, and the spirit aligned in their silent labor of renewal.

Transmutation was the first and fiercest. It is the alchemy of the body, the conversion of what has been bound into what can flow. For decades, I carried grief like sediment in the riverbed of my muscles, rage like static in the circuitry of my nerves. Talk could not reach it. Insight could not dissolve it. The intellect, fluent in narratives, was illiterate in sensation. And so the work began where words end—in the tremor, the gasp, the sob that erupts when the body is given permission to do what it was built to do: release. Breath-work was my doorway. In those sessions, my hands shook, my jaw quivered, my spine writhed like something ancient stirring from hibernation. At first, I feared its violence, mistaking liberation for danger. But as I surrendered, I understood: this was not a breakdown. It was a breakthrough. The kinetic discharge of potential energy hoarded for years, a reclamation of flow that no theory could manufacture. Science affirms what mystics have always known: trauma is not only psychological; it is somatic, encoded in motor patterns, lodged in fascia, inscribed in the autonomic nervous system. To heal is to complete the actions once aborted, to finish the gestures frozen by terror, to let the body speak the language it was silenced from speaking.

Yet transmutation, though necessary, is not sufficient. What rises after the storm of release is a quiet so vast it can feel like emptiness. Here begins **transcendence**—not an escape from embodiment but an expansion within it, a shift from identification with the wound to identification with the witness. In this phase, awareness unfurls like dawn across terrain once shadowed by survival. The mind, accustomed to rehearsing pain, begins to loosen its grip, and in that loosening, perception widens. You see the old narratives for what they are: adaptive fictions, strategies that once safeguarded life but now strangle it. Neuroscience calls this neuroplasticity—the brain's capacity to prune pathways of fear and cultivate circuits of trust. But beneath the clinical frame lies a sacred truth: transcendence is the birth of choice, the reclamation of agency from reflex. It is the moment you realize that while you cannot rewrite the past, you can stop reliving it in the theater of the present.

And when transmutation and transcendence converge, something subtler, slower, more enduring begins to take root: **transformation**. Not the sudden metamorphosis we romanticize, but the incremental weaving of a new pattern through daily gesture and granular decision. Transformation is not dramatic; it is devotional. It unfolds in the way you breathe when panic knocks again and you no longer collapse beneath its weight. In the way you speak when anger flares, you choose clarity over combustion. In the way you rise each morning to repeat the rituals that remind your cells of safety, your heart of coherence, your mind of silence. Over time, these micro-shifts aggregate into a new baseline, a frequency calibrated not to fear but to flow. And in that resonance, life no longer feels like a gauntlet of threats but a continuum of invitations—to feel, to witness, to become.

Conscious Awareness: The True Home

If I were to name the single thread that stitched these processes together, it would be awareness—not as a concept, but as the felt presence that remained when every identity unraveled. Awareness is not an achievement. It is not manufactured by effort or conferred by mantra. It is what remains when effort ceases, when the machinery of striving grinds to stillness and the self, exhausted by its own performance, collapses into the arms of what it has always fled: the Now. For me, this recognition did not bloom in a monastery or under the tutelage of a sage. It emerged in the raw theater of panic, when every strategy failed and silence became the only terrain left to inhabit. In that silence, I discovered a witnessing that neither clung nor condemned, a presence vast enough to hold terror without drowning in it. That presence was not separate from me, yet it was not what I had called "me." It was older than thought, deeper than feeling, spacious enough to contain both without becoming either.

Neuroscience glimpses fragments of this mystery when it maps the quieting of the default mode network during meditation or the surge of gamma waves in states of deep absorption. But graphs cannot capture the intimacy of this meeting—the moment you realize that you are not the storm but the sky in which the storm unfurls. From this vantage, healing ceases to be a conquest and becomes a conversation, a dialogue between awareness and the phenomena that arise within it. Thoughts appear and dissolve like ripples on a lake. Emotions surge and subside like tides. And through it all, the witness remains untouched, unscarred, serenely luminous.

Living from this awareness does not sterilize life of pain. It does not anesthetize grief or exile anger. What it does is soften the tyranny of identification. You feel without fastening. You suffer without becoming the suffering. You love without chaining the beloved to your need. In this spaciousness, compassion blooms—not as moral obligation but as the natural fragrance of freedom. And from that fragrance flows a way of being that no trauma can extinguish: presence, unadorned and immeasurable.

Closing Reflection: Welcome Home

What began as a collapse has become a compass. The panic that once mocked my strength became the portal through which I walked into a life I did not know was possible—a life not devoid of struggle but devoid of pretense, a life where the metrics of worth have dissolved into the immediacy of breath, the quiet sacrament of being. If there is an arrival, it is not to a destination but to a dimension, the dimension of awareness that was here before the first wound and will remain after the last scar fades. To dwell in that dimension is to know that you were never broken, only fragmented by forgetting. And to remember is to come home—not to the self you once were, not to the future self you imagine, but to the witness that has never moved, the still point around which all becoming turns.

So pause now. Let the words recede like tidewater. Inhale slowly, exhale gently, and feel the silence that hums beneath the syntax. That silence is you. That awareness is the hearth you have sought across decades of detours. You are home.

Chapter Ten
Perception vs. Perspective

> **"You are not a drop in the ocean.**
> **You are the entire ocean in a drop."**
> — *Rumi*

We have walked through fire. We have felt our bones shake under the weight of old wounds, sat inside the furnace of transformation when everything familiar fell apart, and learned to breathe when breath was the only anchor left. We have stilled the storm long enough to feel the mind quiet and the body release what it carried for years in silence. We have touched awareness—not as an idea, but as an experience—and in that touch, remembered something ancient, something unbreakable beneath the mask we thought was who we were.

And now, we begin to live. But how we live—and how we experience one another—will depend on one essential ability: our capacity to distinguish between **perception** and **perspective**.

Perception is primal. It is the body's first language, the way the nervous system interprets reality through our five senses—sight, sound, taste, smell, touch—and then shapes that raw input through the filters of memory and meaning. It is fast, immediate, and deeply instinctual. It is not just what your eyes see or your ears hear; it is the story your body whispers before your mind can even speak. Every detail is colored by what came before. A sudden movement. A raised voice. Even the tone of a text message—all of it filters through layers of personal history, through patterns carved into the nervous system long before today.

This is why two people can step into the same room and feel two entirely different worlds. One hears laughter and feels warmth. Another hears the same laughter and feels exclusion. Nothing in the present moment changed—the difference lives in the internal archive of experience. Perception is not truth. It is an interpretation. It is a mirror polished by trauma, by repetition, by inherited beliefs that often are not even our own. Neuroscience confirms this: the brain does not process reality as it is—it reconstructs reality from fragments, matching what it senses against what it remembers. Every glance, every sound, every smell becomes a negotiation between now and then.

Perspective, on the other hand, belongs to consciousness. It is the space that opens between stimulus and response, the breath that loosens the grip of immediacy. Perspective is not given—it is chosen. It is the quiet vantage point that allows us to step outside the storm of our own thoughts and see from another lens. Where perception says, *"This is happening to me,"* perspective whispers, *"Something is happening—and I can choose how to meet it."*

Perception is reactive. Perspective is reflective. Perception locks us into survival. Perspective invites us into leadership. Perception isolates. Perspective connects.

And this difference is not poetic. It is biological. Perception is tied to the sympathetic nervous system—the fight-flight-freeze circuitry designed to keep us alive. When it senses a threat, it narrows the field of vision, sharpens hearing for danger, floods the bloodstream with cortisol, and primes muscles for defense. This worked beautifully when predators roamed and safety was a matter of seconds. But when your body responds to an email like it's a saber-toothed tiger, that same brilliance becomes a burden. The body cannot tell the difference between a real threat and a remembered one. It responds to vibration, to tone, to subtle energetic cues—and most of those cues live inside us long before they appear outside of us.

This is why perception is powerful—and dangerous. A nervous system trained by trauma will misread safety as threat, intimacy as risk, and silence as punishment. It will summon survival strategies—rage, withdrawal, control—not because we are broken, but because our biology is loyal. It will do whatever it must to keep us alive, even if it costs us love, peace, and connection.

Perspective changes this. When you pause, when you breathe, when you create that fractional gap between feeling and acting, something extraordinary happens: your brain shifts states. The amygdala—the alarm center—begins to quiet. The prefrontal cortex—the seat of reason and empathy—switches on. The heart rate slows. The vagus nerve hums like a tuning fork, signaling safety. In that space, you are no longer the echo of your past—you are the presence of your now. And presence is power.

When we live unaware of this difference, we are trapped in a hall of mirrors, mistaking projection for reality. We think we are seeing the world as it is, when in truth, we are only seeing the vibration of our own unhealed fear reflected back to us. But when we learn to pause, to regulate, to shift from perception into perspective, everything changes. We begin to wonder, *What is this person carrying that I cannot see? What wound is speaking through their words? What survival pattern is being played out right now—not just in them, but in me?*

That wonder—that widening—is wisdom. And wisdom is what makes us better leaders, partners, parents, and human beings.

This chapter is the final movement of everything we've explored—not because the journey is over, but because the journey is finally being lived. Applied. Embodied. And it begins where every story of transformation begins and ends—with the body.

Reactions: The Nervous System in Motion

Most of us do not realize when we are reacting. We believe we are choosing, deciding, and leading with intention. But beneath the surface, most of what we call choice is choreography set in motion years ago. We are not choosing—we are protecting. Defending. Bracing against echoes only we can hear.

A reaction is not an act of will. It is an act of memory. It is the nervous system moving faster than thought, replaying instructions coded in moments of overwhelm. The raised voice in an argument. The email fired off too quickly. The withdrawal when someone steps too close. The anxiety that flares when plans change. The tightness in your chest when someone says, "We need to talk." These are not flaws in character—they are survival patterns written into muscle and fascia, rehearsed until they feel like personality.

Neuroscience tells us the body holds the score of every experience we've endured. Unprocessed pain is not abstract—it is electrical, chemical, cellular. Trauma embeds not only in the mind but in the body's tissues, in the very wiring of the autonomic nervous system.

And without conscious interruption, those loops play on repeat. A slammed door becomes a childhood fight. A boss's critique becomes a parent's disapproval. A partner's silence becomes abandonment. Perception misfires, and the body obeys the memory, not the moment.

This is why reactions feel bigger than the situation at hand. They are not about now—they are about then. And here is the deeper truth: those reactions are not just yours. They are ancestral. Generational. Studies in epigenetics show trauma can alter gene expression, meaning fear patterns are passed down like heirlooms. The anger you can't explain, the hypervigilance that never leaves—these may not have started with you. They may have started three generations back, carried in blood and breath, humming beneath your skin like an old frequency. When you react, you are often vibrating to music you didn't choose.

This is why perception alone is not enough. If you stay in perception, you stay in the echo. You keep transmitting the same frequency into every room you enter. But when you notice the pull of reactivity, when you pause and name it, you disrupt the loop. You move from automatic perception to conscious perspective. And in that shift, you change more than your own story—you change the lineage. You interrupt patterns that have been cycling for decades, maybe centuries. That is the weight and wonder of awareness.

So the next time you feel the heat rise, the chest tightens, and the jaw clenches, remember this: You are not failing. You are receiving data. A reaction is an invitation to trace the thread back to its origin, to feel what was unfelt, to bring light to what was buried. That is where emotional intelligence begins—not with control, but with curiosity.

And the bridge to that curiosity is stillness.

Stillness: The Space Where Truth Arrives

If reaction is the echo of the past, then stillness is the voice of the present. Stillness is not the absence of movement—it is the presence of awareness. It is the nervous system finding a different rhythm, shifting from the staccato of survival into the steady hum of safety.

Stillness is not about silence in the external world; it is about the silence you cultivate inside the storm. It is not the long hours spent in meditation—though they may steady the mind—but the instant you witness the old pattern surface and decide, with quiet defiance, not to bow to it. It is the breath that interrupts the spiral. The pause before the text is sent. The heartbeat you listen to instead of the story you want to scream. In that pause, vibration changes. The frequency of fear begins to dissolve, and the nervous system tunes to something softer. Stillness recalibrates the entire field—heart rate slows, cortisol drops, coherence emerges. This is not philosophy; this is physiology meeting energy. Science meeting spirit.

Stillness births perspective. It creates the space where clarity lands like a feather instead of crashing in like a wave. Without stillness, we live in perpetual reaction, mistaking motion for progress. We hustle, we fix, we speak without listening, and we call it leadership. But leadership without stillness is just control in disguise. Parenting without stillness becomes domination. Love without stillness becomes performance.

In stillness, you don't escape your reactions—you meet them with open eyes. You feel the urge to run, and you stay. You hear the ego's argument, and you choose silence. You become the witness to your own storm. And in that witnessing, you remember: *I am not this noise. I am the sky it moves through.*

From here, everything shifts. In business, stillness looks like listening before leading, depth over speed, clarity over chaos. In relationships, it sounds like breath between words, presence before performance. In parenting, it feels like a lowered voice when you want to raise it, a gentle question instead of a command. Stillness is not weakness. It is mastery. It is the quiet force that turns reaction into response and perception into perspective.

When stillness becomes your baseline, urgency loses its grip. Fear loosens its teeth. You stop vibrating at the frequency of chaos and start resonating with coherence. And coherence—the alignment of mind, body, and heart—is the foundation of wisdom.

From this place, you can act—not from fear, but from freedom, not from old echoes, but from new choices. And that is the essence of power. Real power.

The kind that needs no performance, because presence speaks louder than force.

Business & Leadership

In business, perception often masquerades as decisiveness. We celebrate quick thinking, instinctual calls, and leaders who seem unshakable in the storm. From boardrooms to startups, we are taught to move fast, to "trust the gut," to deliver answers before the question is even fully asked. But rarely do we stop to ask: what is this gut instinct built on? What if the instinct we glorify is not clarity but conditioning? What if the speed we worship is not wisdom but survival?

Here's the truth: most leaders are not responding to the present—they are reacting from their past. What feels like confidence may, in reality, be urgency born from fear. What looks like control may be the nervous system bracing against chaos it once knew too well. Neuroscience explains this with startling precision: under stress, the prefrontal cortex—the brain's center for reasoning and empathy—goes offline, while the amygdala, our alarm system, takes command.

Leadership decisions made from this state are not visionary; they are defensive. They are perception, not perspective.

And perception can poison an organization. A leader who feels threatened—even subconsciously—will misinterpret curiosity as challenge, innovation as risk, and feedback as defiance. Their tone hardens. Their presence sharpens. The frequency they emit—because make no mistake, leadership is energetic—drops into fear, and everyone feels it. Teams may not have the language for vibration, but they sense the tension in their bones. They mirror it through mirror neurons, the same neural circuits that allow us to empathize, to "feel" another's state in our own body. In other words, your nervous system trains the nervous systems of those you lead.

When fear hums beneath the surface, trust withers. A silent room is often not a harmonious room—it is a fearful one. And fear does not innovate. Fear does not create cultures of collaboration. Fear breeds compliance at best and collapse at worst.

This is why awareness is the cornerstone of conscious leadership. Awareness interrupts the autopilot. It calls the leader back from the edge of reactivity into the ground of presence. Presence changes everything because presence carries coherence—a vibrational state where mind, heart, and body align. When a leader enters a room, regulated and rooted, their very physiology sends a message: *It is safe to speak. It is safe to be seen.* This is not motivational theory; this is biology. Research on psychological safety shows that teams perform exponentially better when they feel secure to share ideas without fear of punishment. And that security begins not with policy—but with energy.

Think about the last leader who inspired you. Was it their title that moved you? Their salary? Or was it their steadiness? Their ability to remain calm when everything shook? That calm was not accidental—it was cultivated. Conscious leaders do not wait for peace to find them; they practice creating it inside themselves so they can transmit it to others.

I learned this lesson long before I had the language for it. During my time in the military, leadership wasn't a buzzword; it was survival. And one of the most powerful lessons didn't come from a manual or a mission—it came from a ritual so simple it almost went unnoticed: leaders ate last. Always. Junior soldiers went first, then the ranks above them, and only when everyone had been served did the highest-ranking leaders step forward. It wasn't about food. It was about frequency. About sending an embodied message: *I am here for you. I protect you. Your well-being is my priority.* That act recalibrated the energy of the entire unit. It built trust not through speeches, but through service.

The corporate world could learn something from that. Leadership is not about commanding from the top—it is about anchoring from the center. It is about lowering the vibration of fear so that others can rise into creativity, courage, and contribution. It is about trading control for connection, domination for dialogue, ego for empathy.

And when mistakes happen—and they will—reactive cultures punish, hide, and deflect. Conscious cultures pause, inquire, and learn. They see failure not as a verdict but as feedback. They recognize that accountability, when infused with perspective, becomes a force for growth, not shame. This is the frequency of leadership that transforms companies from profit-driven machines into purpose-driven ecosystems. Not because it sounds good in a slogan but because it is the only way humans truly thrive—through safety, trust, and resonance.

Education & Personal Development

Education, in its most conventional form, has been obsessed with performance. Memorize this. Master that. Pass the test, collect the grade and move to the next rung of the ladder. And yet, for all its emphasis on information, education rarely asks the deeper question: *What state of mind and body is this student in as they learn?* Because here is the unspoken truth: learning is not purely cognitive—it is biological. It is vibrational. The nervous system either opens to receive or closes to protect. And no amount of curriculum can penetrate a system locked in survival.

Stress shrinks the brain's capacity to learn. When cortisol floods the bloodstream, neuroplasticity—the brain's ability to form new connections—diminishes. This is why students who feel unsafe, unseen, or shamed often underperform, no matter how intelligent they are. It is not a question of potential; it is a question of regulation. Safety is the soil of growth. Fear is the poison. If you want to ignite true learning, you cannot only teach the mind—you must calm the body. You must create an atmosphere that vibrates at the frequency of curiosity, not judgment.

I witnessed this truth in my own classroom. I taught adult immigrants who were navigating a new language and, for many, a new life. Their courage humbled me daily. But courage does not erase fear. Some students carried exhaustion from overnight shifts, others the invisible weight of starting over in a world that spoke a language they did not yet understand. And what I saw, again and again, was this: when their nervous systems were on high alert, no grammar lesson could land. Words evaporated. Memory collapsed. The body said, "Not safe," and the mind obeyed.

So I learned to pause the drills. To abandon the rigid pace of the textbook. Instead, I taught them what no traditional curriculum included: the body's response to stress. I explained the fight-flight-freeze loop. I told them why their hearts raced during speaking exercises, why their voices trembled. It wasn't stupidity. It wasn't a failure. It was survival. And when they understood that—when they realized their anxiety was not a verdict on their worth but a signal from their biology—the atmosphere shifted. Shoulders softened. Breathing deepened. And with safety came voice. Their sentences were imperfect, but their energy was free. That freedom—that vibrational release—was the real learning.

This is what conscious education looks like. It is not just about transferring knowledge; it is about transforming the state from which knowledge is received. It understands that before we can teach someone what to think, we must teach them how to feel safe enough to think at all. This principle does not only apply in classrooms. It belongs in boardrooms, in families, in every space where human growth is possible.

Personal development suffers from the same illusion as education: the illusion that progress is measured by accumulation—more books, more courses, more hacks. We chase transformation as if it were a finish line, forgetting that real evolution is not about speed but about depth. It is not about stacking practices but about softening patterns. About noticing the vibration beneath the doing. Because if your personal growth is driven by the same survival energy you are trying to escape, you will simply recreate the cycle in a prettier disguise.

Growth without awareness becomes another race. Growth with awareness becomes liberation.

Family & Parenting

Parenting is often described as a responsibility, a duty, a role we step into for the sake of our children. But the deeper truth is this: parenting is a mirror, and it reflects with unflinching honesty. It does not simply show us our love; it reveals our triggers. It surfaces the fears we thought we buried, the patterns we swore we'd never repeat, the wounds we've carried since childhood and disguised as strength. To raise a child is to be confronted daily by the parts of ourselves we have not yet healed.

This is why parenting feels so overwhelming at times—not because our children are broken, but because they awaken in us the memories of what it felt like to be small, powerless, unseen. Every tantrum, every slammed door, every defiant glance can stir echoes of a time when *we* were silenced, punished, or dismissed. Without awareness, we will not parent from intention, but from instinct. Not from perspective, but from perception.

Most people parent the way they were parented. Not because they choose to, but because the nervous system defaults to what it knows. This is the unconscious inheritance of trauma: patterns passed down not through malice, but through memory—through the wiring of survival. Were you yelled at as a child? Your nervous system learned that yelling equals control. You were ignored when you cried? Your body learned that emotions are unsafe, that expression equals rejection. These lessons become your baseline frequency, and unless you interrupt the loop, that frequency will reverberate through your home, shaping the nervous systems of your children.

Consider what science reveals: the first eight years of life are the most formative. During this window, a child's brain operates primarily in theta waves—a state of deep impressionability. They absorb not only words, but energy. They feel the vibration beneath your tone, the truth beneath your reassurance, the tension behind your smile. You can tell a child, *"Everything is fine,"* but if your body hums with anxiety, they will learn anxiety. They will regulate your dysregulation because co-regulation is their only option. They are not just listening—they are tuning in.

This is why conscious parenting begins with self-awareness. It is not about perfection. It is about presence. About noticing the heat rise in your chest before you yell. About pausing long enough to ask: *What is being triggered in me right now? Is this about my child—or about the child I used to be?*

When you ask these questions, you create a gap. And in that gap, the cycle can break. You become the interrupter of patterns that have persisted for generations. You stop vibrating at the frequency of fear and shift into safety. That shift is not just psychological—it is biological. It rewires your nervous system and, by extension, begins to rewire your child's.

Let's speak to something often left unspoken: the masculine and feminine energies within a home. These are not rigid roles, but energetic principles. Masculine energy, at its highest expression, provides structure, stability, and safety. Feminine energy offers nurture, intuition, and flow. When these energies are distorted, imbalance follows. A father who mistakes control for strength creates an atmosphere of fear. A mother who suppresses her own needs in the name of sacrifice breeds silent resentment. Children feel this—even if they cannot name it.

But when these energies harmonize—when the masculine anchors without dominating, and the feminine nurtures without disappearing—children flourish. They learn by example what balance feels like, what love looks like when it is not conditional, what respect sounds like when it is spoken through action. This is not theory. It is vibration. It is the atmosphere of the home that teaches them, long before words ever do, whether the world is a place to fear or a place to trust.

Parenting will break you open. It will reveal the fractures you thought were sealed. But in those fractures lies the invitation: to heal in real time. To show your children what repair looks like. To say, "I was wrong," without drowning in shame. To demonstrate that transformation is possible—not as a performance, but as a lived reality.

Your child does not need a perfect parent. They need an authentic one. They need someone who knows how to pause, how to breathe, and how to choose connection over control. Because in that choice, you teach them the most profound lesson of all: that love is not earned through obedience, but given through presence.

And if you were raised in a home where love was conditional, where punishment felt like domination, where emotional expression was silenced—hear this: you have the power to end that lineage. You are the pattern-breaker. The one who says, "It stops with me." And in doing so, you alter not only your child's life but the vibration of generations yet to come.

Addiction, Recovery & Mental Health

Addiction has long been misunderstood as a defect of character, a failure of willpower, a collapse of morality. But addiction is not a flaw—it is a symptom.

It is not a sign of weakness—it is a sign of pain. Beneath every compulsion, every craving, every destructive habit lives a simple truth: something inside you is hurting, and it has not been heard.

For many, addiction begins as an attempt to feel safe in a world that never felt safe enough. A drink to calm the tremor in the soul. A pill to silence the storm in the mind. A relationship to fill the hollow in the heart. It starts as relief—and ends as a cage. Neuroscience tells us why: addictive substances and behaviors hijack the brain's reward circuitry, flooding it with dopamine, creating surges of pleasure so intense the system rewires itself to chase that spike at any cost. But here is the piece often ignored: the vulnerability to addiction is not random. It is rooted in trauma. In unprocessed pain. In nervous systems conditioned to seek regulation from the outside because they never learned how to create it from within.

This is why addiction is not about the substance—it is about the state. Remove the alcohol, the drug, the behavior, and the pattern, and you will find another outlet—because the need was never for the thing itself. The need was for relief. For a break from the relentless hum of hypervigilance. For a way out of the memories stored like landmines in the body.

I know this because I have lived on the edge of that desperation. I have felt the mind spiral into darkness so dense it seemed impenetrable. I have stood at the cliff of existence, whispering reasons to stay and hearing only echoes in return. For months, suicidal ideation shadowed my every breath. Panic attacks hijacked my days. Emergency rooms became revolving doors, not because my body was failing—but because my nervous system was collapsing under decades of unprocessed weight. Doctors checked my heart. My lungs. My blood. But the real crisis was in my wiring. In the loops of fear and shame and grief that no scan could capture.

That collapse became my initiation—not into death, but into awakening. Because when the old coping strategies fail, when every exit closes, you are left with the only path that leads home: inward. Into the ache. Into the trembling body. Into the breath you once ignored. That descent is terrifying. It feels like unraveling—and it is. But what unravels is not you; it is everything that kept you from you.

Recovery, then, is not about abstinence alone. It is about integration. About remembering who you were before the wound—and who you can become beyond it. It is both biological and spiritual. Biological, because the nervous system must relearn safety, must rewire its response from fight-or-flight to rest-and-digest. Spiritual, because the soul must remember its own worth, its own light, its own unbreakable essence beneath the debris of shame.

This is why the most effective recovery frameworks—like the 12 Steps—are not just about stopping a behavior. They are about surrender. Inventory. Amends. Connection to something greater than self. Each step is a frequency shift, moving you from isolation into resonance, from secrecy into truth, from fragmentation into wholeness. And the beauty of these steps is that they are universal. You need not be addicted to a substance to need it. We are all addicted to something—patterns, personas, approval, avoidance. The path home is the same: awareness, acceptance, alignment.

And here is the invitation I leave you with: what if the craving you've been trying to conquer is not your enemy, but your teacher? What if it is the voice of your nervous system saying, "I need safety"? What if it is the whisper of your soul saying, "I need connection"? When you begin to hear that voice—not with judgment, but with curiosity—you begin to break the spell. You stop abandoning yourself in search of relief. You return, breath by breath, to the body that once betrayed you, only to find it was never the enemy—it was the messenger.

This is recovery. This is healing. Not the absence of pain, but the presence of perspective. Not perfection, but progress. Not conquering the darkness, but learning to walk with light in your hands—even when the night feels endless.

Faith & Spirituality

Faith didn't arrive for me like a sunrise—it came like a storm, and it came when everything else failed. It came when the body broke under years of neglect, when the mind shattered beneath the weight of decades spent performing strength. It came when the nervous system that had carried me through battles, jobs, relationships, and losses finally said, *"Enough."* Faith was not a gift placed in my hands—it was a fire I had to walk through barefoot, bleeding, with no guarantee that anything waited on the other side.

I had spent most of my life looking at faith from the outside. I watched others cling to their rituals and wondered how they believed so easily, how they trusted something invisible while I wrestled with everything I could see. When I reached my lowest point—when suicidal thoughts became my morning prayer and ER visits became my confession booth—I turned to what seemed like the only remaining option: religion. I wanted to be washed clean. I wanted the weight to lift. I wanted peace to find me in the waters of baptism.

At forty years old, I sat in catechism classes like a child hungry for answers. I read the doctrines, memorized the prayers, and tried to keep the doubt with devotion. And when the day came—when holy water ran over my head—I waited for something to happen. For a light to split the sky, for a peace to invade my bones, for the ache to dissolve into grace. But nothing happened. No voice from heaven. No sudden calm. Just ritual. Just water. And still—the ache remained.

That moment broke me open in a different way. Because I realized something that changed everything: I wasn't looking for God. I was looking for safety. I wanted something external to fix what felt fractured inside. I wanted a symbol to erase the shame, a sacrament to silence the storm. But faith, I would learn, does not live in symbols. It does not reside in the architecture of churches or the cadence of chants—not because those things lack beauty, but because they are only gateways. They are maps, not destinations.

Faith is not memorized. It is metabolized.

The deeper I journeyed, the more I understood that faith is not a system you subscribe to—it is a frequency you embody. It is coherence in a world of chaos. It is the nervous system shifting from survival to surrender. Neuroscience confirms what mystics have known for centuries: practices of prayer, meditation, and contemplative silence alter brain chemistry, reducing stress hormones, increasing dopamine and serotonin, and strengthening neural pathways for regulation. But beyond the science lies something subtler: the resonance of presence. When you breathe slowly and whisper, *"I trust,"* your body hums differently. Your vibration rises. Not because your circumstances changed—but because you did.

And when that happens, your perception transforms. You stop seeing life as punishment and start seeing it as preparation. You stop asking, *"Why me?"* and start asking, *"What is this teaching me?"* This shift is not intellectual—it is energetic. It moves through every cell. It turns panic into prayer, not because the panic disappears, but because the presence within it grows louder than the fear.

As I sat in the silence of my own collapse, I began to revisit truths I had skimmed past in earlier years. The gifts of the Spirit—Wisdom, Understanding, Counsel, Fortitude, Knowledge, Piety, and Reverence—sounded like theological jargon once. But in the stillness, they became alive. Wisdom wasn't in books—it was in breath. Understanding didn't come from sermons—it came from sitting with pain until it spoke. Counsel was the whisper of intuition. Fortitude was the nervous system choosing regulation over reaction.

These were not religious abstractions—they were energetic activations.

And then I saw what every tradition has been pointing to: that the divine is not distant. It is not confined to temples or texts. It is not waiting in the sky—it is pulsing in your chest. It breathes when you breathe. It pauses when you pause. The yogis call it Atman. Jesus called it the Kingdom within. Mystics call it the still point. Science calls it coherence. Whatever name you give it, its truth remains: you are not separate from what you seek.

So if you've spent your life searching for God in the stars, wondering why the silence feels endless, hear this: the silence is not empty. It is full of you. And when you drop deep enough into that stillness—beyond the noise of fear, beyond the echo of shame—you don't just believe.

You know.

Prison Systems & Reentry Programs

I have never been incarcerated. I have never lived inside walls where the clocks mock you and the bars dictate your breath. So I approach this conversation with humility, knowing that my understanding is partial, secondhand, and stitched together from the stories of those who have lived it. But I also approach it with reverence—because some of the most profound examples of resilience I've ever seen came from men who chose to awaken in the darkest places imaginable.

During my time as Director of Production at a nonprofit, I worked with men in a rehabilitation program rebuilding their lives after addiction and incarceration. Many of them were fathers desperate to reconnect with children, sons trying to make amends to mothers, brothers determined to rewrite the narrative they had inherited. What struck me wasn't their mistakes—it was their hunger. Their hunger for redemption, for dignity, for a chance to become someone more than their worst moment.

But here's what we rarely talk about: prison is not just a place. It's an ecosystem. A vibrational field steeped in fear, hypervigilance, and survival. In environments like that, the nervous system never rests. Cortisol floods the body daily. Hyperarousal becomes the baseline. And when your biology is screaming "danger," reflection feels impossible. Closing your eyes for a breath can feel like a risk. Stillness can feel unsafe.

This is why telling someone in prison to "just meditate" can sound naive. On the surface, it feels detached from the crushing reality of confinement, where silence is weaponized and stillness is rare. And yet, stories continue to emerge—of people who, against all odds, find peace in the midst of chaos. Who learn to breathe through panic in cells no bigger than closets. They teach each other not just how to survive but how to soften in a world that punishes vulnerability. That is sacred work. Because it proves something radical: even in a cage, the soul can choose freedom.

Science now affirms what these men intuited: micro-moments of mindfulness can recalibrate the nervous system, even in hostile environments. A single deep breath activates the vagus nerve, signaling safety to the body, lowering heart rate, and easing the grip of fight-or-flight. Does it erase systemic injustice? No. Does it undo decades of trauma? Not overnight. But it creates a crack in the armor. And sometimes, that crack is where the light gets in.

Here's the truth: incarceration doesn't begin with crime. It begins with disconnection. Generational trauma, poverty, and untreated mental illness—these are the breeding grounds of cycles that end behind bars. And if we want to break those cycles, we can't just focus on reentry—we have to focus on re-humanization. We have to remind people of their inherent worth before the world convinces them otherwise. We have to give them tools not just for compliance, but for consciousness.

Breath-work. Journaling. Trauma education. These are not luxuries—they are lifelines. Because freedom is not a date on a calendar. Freedom begins the moment you realize that while they can lock your body, they cannot chain your awareness. And when you reclaim that awareness—when you shift your vibration from fear to presence—you begin to walk out of the mental prison long before the gates swing open.

So if you are reading this from inside those walls—or from the edge of a return—hear me: you are not your sentence. You are not your mistakes. You are not the story the system told about you. You are the moment you choose to breathe, to pause, to remember who you were before the wound and who you can become beyond it. You are the perspective that rises above the perception that says, *"You'll never change."* You are proof that even in the lowest frequency spaces, light can hum. You are living evidence that redemption is not a fantasy—it is a frequency. And it is available now.

Chapter Eleven
The Search for Home

> **"No one saves us but ourselves. No one can and no one may. We ourselves must walk the path."**
>
> — *Buddha*

For years, I wandered—not across landscapes in the traditional sense, though my life carried me through cities and states, jobs and relationships, shifting roles and belief systems—but in the way that is far less visible and far more consuming: the wandering of the soul. It was a kind of quiet homelessness that no amount of stability could mend, the sense that no matter where I stood, I was standing on borrowed ground, as if life itself were a train station where I lingered too long without ever boarding a train.

On the surface, I appeared to function like anyone else. I worked. I smiled. I showed up for life wearing the mask I thought was expected of me. But beneath the surface, there was an emptiness that language struggled to contain—a fracture I could feel but could not name. It was like living in a house with walls that looked solid but echoed hollow when you knocked on them. There was movement, but no arrival. Motion without meaning. A restlessness that felt almost cellular, as though even my bones remembered something I had forgotten.

I searched in the ways I knew how, which is to say, in the ways the world taught me: I set goals. I chased dreams. I built identities like scaffolding, hoping one of them might feel like a home I could finally settle into. And when those efforts failed to quiet the ache, I turned inward. I sat in silence until my legs were numb. I filled notebooks with reflections and questions that circled each other like restless birds. I ran on empty roads, trying to outrun the heaviness lodged inside my chest. I meditated until thoughts blurred at their edges, and still the unease persisted, whispering in the pauses between breaths.

I devoured books. Ancient texts. Modern guides. Words that promised awakening and freedom, words that mapped the architecture of the mind and the subtle pathways of spirit. And some of those words helped, in moments. They gave me glimpses—brief flashes like sunlight breaking through a canopy—but never permanence. Because what I sought could not be read into existence. It had to be remembered.

There were nights I cried until the sound dissolved into silence, and mornings I woke with a hollowness that no amount of prayer or planning could fill. I fasted from distractions. I drowned in them. I practiced breath-work, desperate to inhale peace and exhale whatever darkness clung to me. And for a while, it felt like progress. But sooner or later, the wave of uncertainty would return, crashing against every fragile sense of security I had built.

What was I looking for? Safety. Belonging. A sense of arrival so complete that I could exhale without the fear of what might come next. And though I would not have had the words for it then, what I was truly searching for was home—not a home with walls and windows, but the home that lives inside us, the one untouched by circumstance or time.

Looking back, I understand something I didn't then: this longing wasn't unique to me. It is woven into the human experience, a silent inheritance we all carry. Because somewhere along the way—through trauma, through conditioning, through the systems we're born into—we forget. We forget what it feels like to inhabit ourselves fully, without apology or fear. We learn to perform, to fragment, to fit the shapes demanded of us, and in doing so, we exile the parts of us that feel too tender to show. We leave ourselves long before we leave our childhood homes, and then we spend years, sometimes lifetimes, trying to return without realizing that what we seek isn't lost—it's simply buried beneath layers of forgetting.

Science, in its own language, affirms what mystics have whispered for centuries: the body keeps score. Every moment of unsafety, every unprocessed experience, every heartbreak and humiliation—these do not vanish. They embed themselves in the soft tissue of our being, imprinting on the nervous system, shaping not just our memories but our reflexes, our behaviors, our entire way of relating to the world. And so, even when the danger is gone, the body remains vigilant, scanning for threats, rehearsing old stories in an endless loop.

And here's what makes this even more complex: the mind, restless and relentless, generates an estimated twelve thousand thoughts per day, most of them recycled from yesterday, and the day before, and the years before that. Imagine for a moment trying to navigate that storm consciously. It would be impossible. These thoughts run like background programs on a device—unseen, unheard, yet constantly influencing what we feel, what we choose, who we believe ourselves to be. And still, we cling to the illusion of control, convinced that we are steering the ship when, in truth, the ship often sails itself according to maps we didn't even know were drawn.

This is why I wandered. This is why so many of us wander—not because we lack intelligence or effort or desire, but because no one ever taught us how to become intimate with the inner machinery of our existence. We were taught to chase achievement, to curate identities, to build futures, but never to pause and ask: Who is the one doing all this striving? Who am I beneath the thoughts, beneath the roles, beneath the stories I've carried like scripture?

For most of my life, I didn't ask those questions—not really. I was too busy surviving, too busy trying to fix what I thought was broken, too busy running from the silence that might have answered me sooner. And yet, every failure, every panic attack, every sleepless night was its own kind of teacher, guiding me toward a truth I couldn't yet articulate: that home was never out there. It was here, in the quiet I feared, in the awareness I avoided, in the self I had abandoned.

But I didn't know that then. All I knew was that I was tired—tired of the endless seeking, tired of being a passenger in my own life, tired of chasing a horizon that always receded as I moved closer. I wanted to land, to belong, and I desperately wanted to come home.

The Moment That Changed Everything

It didn't happen the way most turning points do in movies—with a sweeping score, a dramatic setting, and perfect timing. No, it happened in the simplest way possible, on an ordinary day, in a moment so unremarkable it could have easily been missed. I was sitting alone, phone pressed against my ear, speaking to a man whose name I had only recently learned but whose presence, even though a voice carried by invisible signals, felt like something I had been searching for all along.

He wasn't a doctor, though I had spoken to more of those than I could count. He wasn't a preacher, though I had leaned into religion in my desperation for certainty. He was a conscious counselor—someone who didn't offer formulas or quick fixes, but something far rarer: space.

And when I say space, I don't mean silence in the way most people do, the awkward gaps we rush to fill in conversation. I mean a kind of spaciousness that could hold everything I was too tired to keep carrying—the panic attacks, the sleepless nights, the questions that clawed at the edges of my mind like wild animals demanding answers. I mean the kind of listening that makes you feel, perhaps for the first time in your life, that you don't have to edit yourself to be accepted.

That day, my voice shook as I spoke—not because I didn't trust him, but because I didn't trust myself. I had spent years circling the same questions like a bird tethered to an invisible thread, and now, after all the books and therapies and rituals, I still had no clarity. I told him everything, or at least everything I could find words for: the storms that came without warning, hijacking my breath and convincing me I was dying; the nights I paced like a caged animal, trying to outrun thoughts that multiplied faster than I could silence them; the regressions that came during meditation, fragments of images I didn't understand—trains pulling away from stations, pigeons perched like silent judges, landscapes dissolving into a mist I couldn't penetrate.

I told him about the exhaustion, about how even joy felt muted, like sound heard through a wall. And then I said the words that had been swelling inside me for years, the words that carried the weight of everything I couldn't fix:

"I just want to feel safe. I just want to feel at home."

For a moment, the line between us was filled with nothing but the sound of our breathing—mine jagged and shallow, his slow and steady, as if lending me an anchor in the storm. He didn't rush to speak. He didn't give me the usual prescriptions I had grown used to—the mantras, the positive affirmations, the step-by-step guides to happiness. He simply waited, and in that waiting, something in me softened.

And then, his voice came through, calm and warm and disarmingly simple:

"Where do you think home is?"

I froze. Not because I didn't have an answer, but because I had never even considered the question. Home had always felt like something outside me, something conditional, something that lived in other people, other places, other moments I couldn't seem to reach. I swallowed hard and said the only truth I knew:

"I don't have a home. That's what I've been searching for."

Another pause, another breath that seemed to carry centuries of wisdom, and then, in a tone that was both tender and undeniable, he said the sentence that would split my life into before and after:

"You are the home you've been searching for."

The words didn't hit me all at once. They didn't crash like a wave—they unfolded like light creeping into a room that had been dark for years. At first, I wanted to resist, to argue, to explain why that couldn't be true, why I had spent decades proving otherwise. But something in the way he said it—a truth so steady it didn't need to convince—slipped past every defense I had built and sank into the marrow of my being.

And then it happened: not an explosion, but a release. My throat tightened. My eyes burned. And before I could stop it, tears spilled—not the hot, angry tears of frustration, but the soft, trembling tears that come when something inside you finally exhales. It was as if every muscle that had been braced for impact, every nerve wired for survival, began to unclench, whispering, you can rest now.

That single sentence became the key that unlocked a door I didn't know I had been standing behind. And what lay beyond that door wasn't some mystical revelation or otherworldly vision—it was something far simpler and far more profound: the quiet recognition that I had never truly left myself. I had only forgotten.

Science might call this a shift in neural patterns, a rewiring of synaptic pathways, a recalibration of the autonomic nervous system. And maybe it was all of those things. Maybe when a truth resonates that deeply, it does more than move the mind—it moves the body. Cortisol levels drop. Heart rate steadies. The brain shifts from the frantic waves of beta into the calm rhythm of alpha. The parasympathetic nervous system, long exiled, returns like a long-lost friend. In other words, safety becomes embodied—not because the world outside changed, but because something inside remembered.

I hung up that phone knowing nothing had changed and everything had. The debts were still there. The wounds were still tender. The future was still uncertain. But for the first time in years, I didn't feel like I was drowning in a life I couldn't control. I didn't feel like a passenger drifting from station to station, searching for a home I could never find. Because in that moment, I understood—home wasn't out there. It was here, in the breath I had been overlooking, in the presence I had been avoiding, in the self I had been running from.

That sentence didn't solve my problems. It didn't erase my pain. But it shattered the illusion that I was lost. And when that illusion fell, so did everything I thought I knew about who I was and what I needed. For the first time, I wasn't asking, when will I arrive? I was whispering, almost in disbelief, I'm already here.

The Science of Awareness & the Hidden Operating System

When the call ended that day, I remember sitting there in silence, phone still in my hand, staring at nothing in particular, as if the entire world had been rearranged in an instant. The words—You are the home you've been searching for—did not linger as an idea to be dissected, but as a truth my body had always carried, waiting only to be remembered. And the more I sat with it, the more I began to see what had been hiding in plain sight all along: the real problem was never that I was lost. The real problem was that I had been living in a system I didn't even understand—a system running me instead of the other way around.

If that sounds abstract, let me break it down. Science tells us the human mind processes roughly twelve thousand thoughts per day, some studies say even more. Twelve thousand. Think about that for a second. If you tried to consciously manage all of them, you'd lose your mind—literally. You'd burn out in minutes because the human brain isn't designed for that level of conscious micro-control. And yet, those thoughts don't disappear just because you're not paying attention. They run like background programs on a phone or computer, unseen but always active, shaping the way you feel, the choices you make, and the reality you believe is yours.

It's like carrying a smartphone in your pocket. You open the screen and see a few apps, maybe a browser or a message thread, but behind that polished surface, dozens of processes are happening—software updates, notifications, system refreshes. You don't see them, you don't control them, and yet they're consuming energy, dictating the performance of the whole device. Your mind is no different. While you're focused on answering an email or having a conversation, there's an entire network of subconscious scripts running in the background: old memories looping like reruns, conditioned responses firing like default settings, beliefs you didn't choose whispering instructions you didn't approve.

And here's the uncomfortable truth: most of us live our entire lives this way, thinking we're the ones in charge, when in reality, our days are governed by patterns so deeply ingrained we rarely question them. We wake up, scroll through the feed of our mind without realizing it, and call it free will. We think we're choosing, but more often than not, we're reacting—reacting to thought patterns installed long before we were aware enough to give consent.

Now, if you're wondering whether that makes us powerless, I understand. That's what I wondered too. If twelve thousand thoughts are firing every day without my permission, what chance do I have? Am I just a passenger in my own head, strapped in for a ride I can't steer? At first glance, it feels that way. And maybe that's why so many of us feel the quiet desperation we do—because somewhere deep down, we sense the truth: we've been running an operating system no one taught us how to navigate.

I often think about this when I look at the way society is structured. From the time we're children, we're taught how to add and subtract, how to memorize history dates and balance equations, but no one teaches us how to observe the mind. No one says, here's how thoughts work. Here's how to notice them without drowning in them. Here's how to create space between what you think and who you are. Instead, we're given scripts—do this, don't do that—and left to assume that the voice in our head is us. And maybe, just maybe, that's not an accident. Maybe awareness was never emphasized because unconscious people are easier to shape, easier to sell to, easier to keep inside systems designed to profit from their distraction.

But here's the part I want you to hear: while you can't stop thousands of thoughts from arising, you can decide what relationship you want to have with them. You can't shut down the operating system, but you can learn how to work with it instead of being ruled by it. And that begins with awareness—not as a concept, but as a living practice, a muscle you strengthen by noticing what has always been there.

Because the truth is, most of the suffering we experience doesn't come from what happens to us; it comes from the unexamined chatter that interprets those events. It comes from believing every thought as if it were gospel, when in reality, thoughts are just electrical impulses dressed in language, flickering in and out like fireflies in the night. Awareness is what lets you see that. Awareness is the light that reveals the wiring of the mind, the silent witness that notices the programs running without judgment, without panic, without the compulsion to control what doesn't need controlling.

And here's where it gets interesting: when you begin to cultivate that awareness, the system starts to shift—not because you force it to, but because observation itself is transformative. In neuroscience, this is neuroplasticity. The brain rewires based on where attention goes. Every time you notice a thought without clinging to it, you're carving a new pathway, weakening the old ones that kept you stuck in loops of fear and self-doubt. You're reclaiming energy that was once trapped in unconscious patterns and redirecting it toward presence, creativity, and peace.

Think about that: twelve thousand thoughts, most of them on autopilot, and yet one simple shift—choosing to observe instead of obey—can begin to change everything. That's not a small thing. That's liberation disguised as stillness.

And maybe you're wondering, if awareness is so powerful, why isn't everyone practicing it? The answer is simple: because it's invisible. Awareness doesn't shout. It doesn't flood you with dopamine like a notification or make promises like a self-help trend. Awareness is quiet, and we live in a world that worships noise. So we miss it. We overlook it. And in doing so, we overlook ourselves.

But now you know. And knowledge carries responsibility. You can't unknow this. You can't go back to believing that every thought is truth, that every reaction is inevitable, that every feeling defines you. You've seen behind the curtain, and what you do with that seeing is what will shape the rest of your life.

Because here's the reality: the system isn't going away. The thousands of thoughts will keep coming. The background processes will keep running. But you are not those processes. You are the awareness in which they arise and dissolve, the still point around which the storm spins. And the more you remember that, the more the illusion of chaos begins to crumble.

So start here. Not by trying to empty your mind—that's a myth and a trap—but by noticing. By watching the play without getting lost in the script. By asking, with gentle curiosity: Who is the one observing these thoughts? Who is the awareness in which they move?

That question is the doorway. Step through it often enough, and you'll begin to see what I finally saw: that home was never something I had to find. It was something I had to wake up to.

And when you begin to wake up, even a little, you start to notice something else: the quality of your conversations begins to change. You start to see that most dialogues aren't really about truth—they're about programming, about people defending the belief systems they've mistaken for themselves. And that realization? That's where we're going next.

Conversations, Consciousness, & Frequencies

As I began to sit more with awareness, something else came into view—something so obvious, yet so easily missed when life is running on autopilot. It was this: the way we communicate and the way we speak to one another, which is a direct reflection of the level of consciousness we're operating from. And once you see this, you can't unsee it. You start noticing how almost every conversation happening around you—on street corners, in boardrooms, over dinner tables—isn't really about truth. It's about patterns. About programming. About vibrations colliding without recognition of what's really happening underneath.

Think about the last conversation you had. Was it about an event? Something that happened, something someone did or said? Most conversations are. Someone tells a story, we respond with judgment or agreement, and we pass opinions back and forth like cards in a game. It sounds like a connection, but look closely and you'll see what's missing: there's no system here. No real method for resolution, no foundation for understanding. Just loops of reaction, fed by unexamined thoughts and feelings.

Let me make this concrete. Imagine this: you tell me your partner forgot your anniversary. You say, "I can't believe he didn't remember. After everything we've been through." And I respond, "Wow, that's awful. I can't believe he did that." You nod. "I know, right?" And we keep going, circling the event like vultures over a carcass—dissecting what happened, replaying it, feeding the narrative. But does it resolve anything? No. Because we're focused on the surface: the event, the behavior, the storyline.

Now, what if we shifted the frame? What if, instead of dissecting the event, we explored the feeling underneath? "How did that make you feel?" I ask. And suddenly, the energy changes. We're no longer looping in blame or justification. We're touching something real: the tenderness, the longing, the fear. That's a different kind of conversation. Or we could go even deeper—past the feelings, into the beliefs driving them, into the subconscious stories that shape what you expect from love and why. That's where transformation begins.

But here's the challenge: most people never get there. Because most of us don't ask what kind of conversation we're having. We just react. We move from thought to word to argument without pausing to notice the architecture of what's happening. And so, we stay trapped—not because the other person is wrong, but because neither of us knows how to step outside the loop.

I learned this the hard way. When my health collapsed and panic attacks hijacked my life, my conversations were almost entirely biological. I spoke the language of symptoms and prescriptions. My sentences were strung together with words like serotonin, neurotransmitters, dosage, and side effects. Doctors were my saviors, and ER visits were my confessions. I prayed at the altar of biology because, at the time, it was the only framework that made sense. If something was broken, there had to be a chemical fix.

But then came psychology. I graduated from biology and entered the world of mindsets and high-performance habits. Suddenly, my conversations were about cognition and behavior, limiting beliefs, and neuro-linguistic programming. I devoured books, watched videos, and attended seminars where the mantras promised to rewire my brain and unlock potential. And for a while, I believed they would.

Then spirituality arrived, uninvited but insistent. My language shifted again. I started talking about energy, chakras, shamans, and rituals under full moons. I swapped science journals for sacred texts, meditation cushions for therapy chairs. And then, as life twisted deeper into pain, I slid into a psychiatric spiral. My words turned heavy with diagnoses, my sentences laced with clinical terms I clung to like lifeboats. None of it worked. Not the pills, not the prayers, not the promises.

Eventually, I tried religion. I baptized myself, thinking maybe redemption lived in holy water. I memorized verses, spoke in absolutes, convinced myself that surrender meant silence, that faith meant obedience. But when the pills betrayed me and the prayers fell flat, I was left staring at the raw truth: none of these languages could give me what I was looking for.

So I quit. I quit everything. I stopped chasing, stopped performing, stopped speaking in borrowed tongues. And in that stillness, I found something I had been running from all along: the voice within. A voice that didn't shout, didn't demand, didn't condemn. A voice that whispered, steady and patient: You are home.

It was around that time that physics entered the frame, not as a subject to study, but as a revelation. Suddenly, the words that once felt abstract—energy, vibration, frequency—clicked into place like the final pieces of a puzzle. I realized these weren't just poetic metaphors for life. They were the architecture of reality. Everything vibrates. Everything moves in frequency. And conversations? They're no different.

Because here's what I know now: every dialogue is an exchange of energy, a collision of frequencies. When you argue with someone, you're not just trading words—you're vibrating at different rates, broadcasting on different channels. That's why it feels like static. That's why no one hears. A religious person may not speak the language of science. A scientist may not understand the tongue of the spirit. Not because either is wrong, but because they're tuned to different frequencies.

This is why I ask myself, every time I step into a conversation, especially when it's charged: What kind of conversation am I having? What language is this? Biological? Psychological? Spiritual? Religious? Somatic? Philosophical? That question is a compass. It helps me level with the person before me, not to agree, but to understand. Understanding changes, the entire frequency of a dialogue, opening a channel where, before, there was only noise.

And here's the paradox: when you see this, you stop needing to be right. You stop trying to force your signal into someone else's bandwidth. You start listening—not to reply, but to recognize. And that recognition? That's where awareness deepens. That's where presence replaces performance. That's where you stop arguing with the world and start harmonizing with it, one frequency at a time.

But there's another layer to this, one that goes even deeper than language or logic. It's the layer of belief systems—the invisible architecture of the mind that determines not just what we say, but what we're even capable of hearing. And until we understand that, we'll keep mistaking noise for truth, mistaking disagreement for danger, mistaking diversity of perspective for war.

Systems of Belief vs. Expanding Awareness

The more I observed conversations—mine and others—the more I realized something that changed everything: most disagreements aren't really about truth. They're about programming. About systems of belief running like software so deep that people don't even know they're operating from them. And until we understand this, we'll keep fighting shadows, thinking we're fighting people.

It's almost tragic when you see it clearly. Two people arguing, each certain they're right, each defending a position as if their life depends on it—because in a way, it does. When your identity is fused to a belief, a challenge to that belief feels like a threat to your existence. That's why the nervous system responds the way it does. Elevated heart rate. Adrenaline surge. Fight-or-flight ignited. Not because the other person is swinging a weapon, but because the mind perceives, if I'm wrong about this, what else am I wrong about? Who am I without this framework?

So we dig in. We defend. We protect. Not because the truth is at stake, but because the self-image built on that truth is. And what's underneath that? Fear. The fear of groundlessness. The fear of not knowing. The fear of dismantling a house of cards we've been living in for decades.

I often think about a clip I once saw—a man standing before a chalkboard covered in equations, teaching physics with passion and precision. The camera cuts to his audience: a baby, sitting in a high chair, staring blankly at the green board. The baby isn't resistant or defiant. The baby is simply incapable of understanding because its brain hasn't developed the capacity yet. And that's what so many of our arguments look like—one person throwing quantum equations at someone whose current level of consciousness is still grasping shapes and colors. And it's not arrogance or ignorance; it's development. And you can't rush development any more than you can force that baby to comprehend particle theory.

Consciousness works the same way. If someone is rooted in a rigid belief system, it's not just that they won't understand you—they can't. Their perception is bound by the limits of the framework they live in. And belief systems are brilliant at self-preservation. They're like armed guards stationed at the gates of awareness, scanning for intruders, ready to shoot down anything that threatens the established order. Because here's the secret no one likes to admit: beliefs aren't about truth. They're about safety. They're about creating a structure that feels solid in a world that is, by nature, fluid.

Think about religion. Think about ideology. Think about even the subtle cultural codes we inherit without question. These systems tell us what's right, what's wrong, what's sacred, and what's profane. They shape our language, our rituals, our sense of identity. And for a while, they serve us. They give us belonging. They give us meaning. But eventually, if growth is your path, they become a cage—a beautifully decorated cage, but a cage nonetheless.

And here's the paradox: the cage isn't locked. The door is open. You could step out anytime. But most people don't. Why? Because the unknown feels scarier than the familiar pain of confinement. Because leaving the cage means confronting the vastness of reality without the comfort of absolutes. And that requires courage—not the courage to fight others, but the courage to dismantle the illusions inside yourself.

So what's the way out? It's not an argument. You can't debate someone into awakening. You can't batter down the walls of a belief system with logic because logic itself is often another wall. The only way out is awareness—because awareness doesn't attack. Awareness observes. Awareness doesn't demand allegiance to a new system; it invites freedom from all systems.

And that's the shift that changed my life. I stopped trying to convert anyone to my point of view and started asking a different question: What level of consciousness am I dealing with here? What is their framework? What is mine? And how can I meet them without losing myself? That question doesn't just dissolve conflict—it expands compassion. It reminds you that everyone is doing the best they can with the map they've been given, and some maps simply don't show the whole territory yet.

But here's the part that hit me hardest: I had to admit that I was no different. I had my own maps, my own guards, my own invisible cages. Every time I clung to certainty, every time I dismissed what I didn't understand, every time I defended a position out of fear, I was just as trapped as the people I judged. And if I wanted to live free—if I wanted to truly come home—I had to do something terrifying. I had to dismantle myself.

I had to let go of the comfort of absolutes. I had to step out of the cage and stand barefoot in the wilderness of not knowing. And when I did, I realized something I'll never forget: the world didn't fall apart when I stopped clinging to my beliefs. It expanded. It opened like a sky unbroken by clouds. Because truth isn't a system you can hold in your hands, it's a presence you awaken to when you stop gripping so tightly.

And that awakening? It begins in the simplest way imaginable—not with force, not with effort, but with a single moment of stillness, a single breath of awareness, a single whisper of curiosity: What else is possible beyond what I've been taught to believe? Ask that question, and you've already cracked the shell. Ask it often enough, and the shell begins to fall away. And when it does, you find yourself standing in a freedom you didn't know existed—the freedom to experience life directly, without filters, without cages, without the constant hum of the operating system running your every move.

But here's the twist: freedom isn't found in rejecting the world. It's found in returning to yourself—not the self built from borrowed beliefs, but the self that existed before the programming, the self that whispers beneath the noise, the self that has been waiting for you to come home.

And that's where we're headed next.

Returning to the Inner Self

There comes a point in every journey where the road you've been running begins to disappear behind you, where the questions that once felt urgent start to lose their edge, and what remains is something so simple, so quiet, that it almost feels like a letdown to the part of you addicted to the chase. That's where I arrived—not in triumph, not in enlightenment, but in exhaustion. I had searched in every direction, scaled every mountain the world told me mattered, spoken in every language of self-improvement, and still, the ache remained.

And then, almost without warning, the question that had haunted me for years—Where do I belong?—was replaced by a different one, softer but infinitely more powerful: What if there's nowhere to go? What if what I've been searching for is already here?

It sounds like a cliché, doesn't it? Everything you need is within you. We've all heard those words slapped across Instagram posts and motivational posters, and they sound lovely—until you're drowning in panic attacks, wondering how your rent will get paid, watching your life unravel thread by thread. When you're in that space, a phrase like that feels less like a truth and more like an insult. If everything I need is within me, then why do I feel like I'm falling apart?

I asked myself that question more times than I can count. And the answer didn't come as a thunderclap of revelation. It came as a whisper in the spaces I had spent years avoiding—the spaces of stillness. Because the truth is, the reason we can't find what's inside us is not that it isn't there. It's that we've built so much noise around it that we can't hear it anymore.

When I finally stopped—really stopped—the truth began to surface, not in words, but in a kind of quiet recognition: everything I had been chasing lived in the awareness that was already holding every experience I had ever had. Awareness is the home we forget because it's too close to notice. It's not a thing you can see because it's the seeing itself. It's not something you can grasp because it's what makes grasping possible.

Think about it: your thoughts, your emotions, your memories, even the sensations in your body—they all come and go. They arise, they pass. They are objects in your field of experience. But what is constant? The awareness that notices them. The silent witness that has been there from the moment you took your first breath to this very instant. That awareness is not local. It doesn't live in your head. It doesn't shrink when your thoughts grow loud or vanish when your mind is still. It is the infinite canvas on which every moment is painted, and you've been looking for the painting instead of recognizing the canvas.

This is what the ancients meant when they said everything is within you. Not that you can think your way to happiness or manufacture peace through effort, but that the core of who you are—the awareness before thought, before identity—is already whole. You don't need to add to it. You just need to uncover it. And that uncovering isn't about doing more. It's about doing less. It's about stillness.

When I say stillness, I don't mean sitting cross-legged on a cushion for hours chanting mantras—though that can help if it calls to you. I mean the simple, radical act of pausing. Of breathing. Of letting the body soften enough for the mind to unclench. Because here's the thing: the mind is like a snow globe in a storm. Shake it hard enough, and you can't see through the swirl of flakes. But set it down, and clarity happens by itself. Stillness is setting the globe down.

Science backs this in ways that feel almost miraculous. When you focus on your breath, when you slow it intentionally, you activate the parasympathetic nervous system—the body's natural brake pedal. Heart rate decreases. Cortisol levels drop. Brain waves shift from frantic beta into the calm hum of alpha and theta, states associated with creativity, clarity, and deep relaxation. Even the heart begins to entrain with the breath, creating coherence between body and mind. And when that happens, the storm inside begins to settle, not because you forced it to, but because that's what happens when you stop feeding it.

This is why breath is the oldest spiritual technology we have. Before there were scriptures, there was breath. Before there were rituals, there was the rise and fall of the lungs, the quiet rhythm that has been with you from the beginning. Every inhale is a reminder that life is still saying yes to you. Every exhale is an invitation to let go of the illusions you've been gripping so tightly.

When I finally embraced this—when I stopped trying to think my way out of suffering and started breathing my way back into the present—I began to experience something I can only describe as a return. A homecoming. Not to a place, but to myself. To the awareness that had been waiting patiently behind the noise of thought, the churn of emotion, and the weight of stories I had mistaken for truth.

And here's the beauty of it: the moment you touch that awareness, even briefly, you realize something that changes everything—you are not your thoughts. You are not your emotions. You are not your history or your habits or the roles you've played. You are the space in which all of that arises and dissolves. You are the awareness that holds it all without being stained by any of it. And once you know that—not as an idea, but as a living experience—the grip of fear begins to loosen. The need to control begins to soften. Because how do you fear what you can see through? How do you cling to what you know will pass?

This doesn't mean life stops challenging you. It doesn't mean pain disappears. It means you meet it differently. You stop drowning in the waves because you've discovered the ocean beneath them—the stillness that doesn't move, no matter how wild the surface becomes.

So if you take nothing else from this, take this: the way home is not out there. It's not in the next achievement, the next relationship, the next spiritual trend. It's here, in this breath, in this moment, in the awareness of reading these words. And the only practice you need—the only one that truly matters—is the practice of remembering.

Because when you remember, even for a second, the entire world begins to shift—not because the world changed, but because you did. And from that shift, everything else becomes possible.

And yet, even with this knowing, there was one more lesson I had to learn before I could truly live free: the lesson of authenticity. The lesson of standing naked in the light of my own truth, no masks, no filters, no apologies. That lesson didn't come easy. It came at a cost I wasn't sure I could pay. But it was the price of freedom, and it was worth everything.

Authenticity: My Last Lesson

I wish I could tell you that once I discovered awareness, once I touched that stillness, everything in my life unfolded in harmony—that the pain dissolved, the chaos settled, and the path ahead was smooth and straight. But that would be a lie. The truth is, life didn't get easier after awakening—it got real. And reality has a way of testing whether the wisdom you claim to hold is more than words, more than concepts, more than something you post about on good days.

For me, that test came like a storm in slow motion. One by one, the things I thought I needed to feel secure began to fall away. First, the job that had anchored my financial stability vanished. Then the cars, symbols of progress and comfort, slipped from my hands. Notices from the court began arriving like uninvited guests, each envelope a reminder that the ground beneath me was shifting faster than I could steady myself. The numbers in my bank account dwindled until all that was left was $15,000—just enough to survive if I played it safe, but not enough to feel anything close to secure.

And in the middle of all this, I made a decision that defied logic: I poured myself into finishing this book. Eight to ten hours a day, for thirty straight days, I wrote—not because I had the luxury of time or resources, but because something in me knew this wasn't just about writing a book. It was about anchoring my truth in a way that couldn't be taken from me. Everything else—status, possessions, certainty—was slipping through my fingers like sand.

But words? Words could build a bridge between who I had been and who I was becoming.

Still, I won't romanticize it. It was brutal. There were nights I lay awake staring at the ceiling, heart pounding with questions that had no easy answers: How long can I hold this together? What happens when the money runs out? Will all of this collapse around me? There were mornings when fear gripped me so tight it felt like a weight pressing on my chest. And in those moments, all the spiritual insights I had collected over the years didn't feel like enough. Awareness? Presence? Breath? Those were easy to practice when life was kind. But now? Now they were being dragged out of theory and into blood and bone reality.

This was the crucible where everything I had learned was tested—not in meditation halls or on retreat, but in the rawness of survival. Could I stay present when every instinct screamed to panic? Could I trust that home was within me when the external world felt like it was crumbling? Could I keep my frequency steady when the vibrations of fear were pounding like drums in my nervous system?

And then came the deeper question, the one that cracked me open in ways I didn't expect: Could I be honest about this? Could I speak it out loud without shame? Could I let the world see me here, stripped of everything society says defines success?

Because here's what I realized: awakening had given me many gifts—clarity, peace, a sense of belonging within—but it hadn't yet given me authenticity. Not fully. I was still carrying masks, still editing my truth to make it digestible, still hiding the parts of me that felt messy, flawed, uncertain. And this season of loss? It burned those masks to ash.

I had to look at myself—not the curated self, not the self-polished for public consumption, but the raw self standing barefoot in the rubble of what used to feel safe. And I had to accept him. Not in some distant future when things looked better, but now. In debt. In doubt. In the silence of nights spent wondering if I had made the biggest mistake of my life. That acceptance felt like death. It felt like letting go of every illusion of control I had left. But on the other side of that surrender, something fierce and liberating rose: authenticity.

Authenticity isn't a trend. It's not about posting your "real" moments for likes or turning vulnerability into a performance. Authenticity is freedom. It's the absence of hiding. It's the courage to look your own darkness in the eye and say, yes, this is me too. It's the power to tell the truth—not the pretty truth, not the filtered truth, but the whole truth—even when your voice shakes, even when you know it might cost you the image you've worked so hard to maintain.

I started speaking differently after that. I stopped pretending I had it all figured out. I told people the truth: that I was broke, that I was scared, that I was betting everything on a vision I couldn't yet see fully. I told them about the court notices, about the cars I lost, about the long nights of wondering if I was crazy for believing this path would lead somewhere meaningful. And you know what happened? The shame that had chained me for years shattered. The fear that had whispered, if they knew, they'd leave, dissolved like smoke. When you speak your truth without apology, you reclaim the energy shame was holding you hostage. You reclaim yourself.

And here's what else happens: your frequency shifts. There's a resonance in truth that nothing else can mimic. When you stop hiding, your body relaxes. Your mind unclenches. Your spirit expands. And people feel it. They may not know why, but they sense the transparency, the integrity, the raw aliveness that comes when you've burned every mask. And in that space, something beautiful unfolds: your authenticity becomes permission for others to do the same.

That's the ripple effect no one talks about. Authenticity doesn't just liberate you—it liberates everyone who touches your energy. It says, without words, you don't have to pretend either. You don't have to hide. And in a world addicted to performance, that is revolutionary.

So if you're here—standing where I stood, stripped of the illusions that once made you feel safe—know this: it's not the end. It's the beginning. It's life asking if you're willing to live unarmored. If you're willing to step into the light with every scar showing. If you're willing to trade perfection for presence.

Say yes. Not because it's easy, but because on the other side of that yes is a freedom so fierce, so unshakable, that nothing external can take it away. And once you taste that freedom, you'll understand what I finally did: that coming home isn't just about finding peace. It's about finding yourself—the whole self, unfiltered, unmasked, unapologetically alive.

The Spectrum of Human Emotion

If there is one thing that reminds us we are human, it is emotion. Emotion colors everything—the way we think, the choices we make, the energy we radiate into the world. And yet, for most of us, emotions are the least understood force in our lives. We treat them like intruders when they hurt, like addictions when they thrill, like mysteries we're too busy to solve. But the truth is, until you understand emotion—what it is, how it moves, and why it arises—you'll never truly feel at home within yourself.

Psychologist Robert Plutchik suggested that humans experience eight primary emotions: joy, sadness, anger, fear, trust, disgust, surprise, and anticipation. Eight sounds manageable, right? But from these eight arise countless variations—shades and blends that multiply into what researchers estimate as 34,000 distinct emotional states. Thirty-four thousand. Imagine walking into a library with 34,000 books and realizing you've only read three. That's what most of us are doing with our inner world. We live in a house with thousands of rooms, but we keep circling the same few hallways, wondering why life feels so small.

Why does this matter? Because emotions are not just feelings—they are frequencies. They are energy in motion, quite literally. When you feel anger, it's not just a mood. It's a biochemical event: cortisol and adrenaline flood your bloodstream, heart rate spikes, muscles tense, and your brain narrows its focus to threat detection. When you feel joy, dopamine and serotonin dance through your neural pathways, expanding your sense of possibility, softening your body, and opening your heart. Emotions tune your entire system, like turning the dial on a radio. And here's the catch: you broadcast the station you're tuned to. Your relationships, your conversations, your opportunities—they all respond to the frequency you emit.

This is why unprocessed emotion is so dangerous. It doesn't just disappear because you ignore it. It lingers, like static in the background, warping your perception, distorting your vibration. You think you're making choices freely, but in reality, you're reacting from old pain, from patterns you don't even remember installing. A childhood wound becomes a filter through which you see every relationship. A betrayal becomes a frequency that hums beneath every conversation. And until you bring that into awareness, you'll keep living the same story, wearing different costumes.

I lived that loop for years without knowing it. Every panic attack I had, every spiral into despair, was my nervous system screaming what my conscious mind refused to hear: Feel this. Don't run. Don't numb. Don't bury. But I didn't know how. No one teaches us this. We're taught math and grammar and how to follow rules, but no one says, here's how to hold grief without drowning. Here's how to meet anger without burning down everything you love. Here's how to feel joy without fearing it will vanish. So we do what we know: we suppress, we distract, we pretend. And every time we do, the body takes the hit. The unprocessed emotion becomes tension in the jaw, tightness in the chest, a knot in the stomach that one day becomes an illness we can't explain.

Here's what changed my life: realizing that emotion is not the enemy. Emotion is information. It's the nervous system delivering a message in a language older than words. Fear says, I need safety. Anger says, I need a boundary. Sadness says, I need to release. Joy says, I am aligned. When you stop labeling emotions as good or bad and start listening to what they're asking for, everything shifts. The storm loses its teeth. The fear becomes a compass instead of a cage.

But listening doesn't mean indulging. It doesn't mean drowning in the story; your mind spins around the feeling. It means creating space. Breathing into the sensation. Observing without judgment, without the rush to fix or flee. This is what awareness makes possible. When you become the witness, you stop being the prisoner. You feel fully, but you don't fuse with the feeling. You let it move through you like a wave—rising, cresting, dissolving—because that's its nature. Every emotion wants one thing: to move.

When you block that movement, you suffer. When you allow it, you heal.

Science confirms what sages have said for centuries: emotions have a lifespan when met with presence. Research shows that the chemical cycle of an emotion lasts about 90 seconds in the body. Ninety seconds. That's how long the wave needs to rise and fall—unless you feed it with thought, unless you grab it and spin a story that keeps the loop alive. That's the trap most of us fall into. The feeling comes, and instead of witnessing it, we narrate it. We turn it into identity: I am angry. I am sad. I am broken. But you are none of those things. You are the awareness holding them. And when you know that—not as an idea, but as a lived experience—freedom begins.

For me, learning this was like discovering a new language. At first, I stumbled. My old habits didn't die quietly. I wanted to run from the heaviness, to be numb with distractions, to drown in work or scroll through screens. But every time I chose to stay—every time I sat in silence and breathed through the tremor in my chest—I felt something shift. The emotions that once felt like tsunamis became waves I could ride. The grief I feared would consume me became a river that cleansed. The anger I thought was a curse became a teacher, pointing me to places where I had abandoned my own boundaries.

And here's the paradox: the more I allowed myself to feel, the lighter I became. Not because the emotions vanished forever, but because they no longer owned me. They passed through like weather instead of moving in like squatters. And with every storm I survived, my trust deepened—not just in myself, but in life. Because I realized something that sounds simple but changes everything: nothing you feel can destroy you when you know who you are beyond what you feel.

That's the gift awareness gives. It doesn't spare you from the human experience—it sanctifies it. It lets you taste the full spectrum without fear because you know the colors don't define the canvas. You know the waves don't shake the ocean. You know the feelings, all 34,000 of them, are guests in the house of your being—not the owner. And when you hold that truth, even the darkest emotions become sacred.

This is what coming home feels like—not a constant state of bliss, but a radical intimacy with whatever arises. Joy, sorrow, rage, tenderness—they all belong. They all have a seat at the table of your humanity. And when you stop exiling them, you stop exiling yourself.

So if you take nothing else from this section, take this: feel everything. Fully. Fiercely. Fearlessly. Not because it's easy, but because it's the doorway. On the other side of feeling is freedom. And on the other side of freedom is love—not the fragile love that depends on conditions, but the unshakable love that is your nature.

And that love? That's what we'll explore as we step into the final part of this journey—the part where all of this integrates into the way you live, breathe, and move through the world. The part where coming home stops being a concept and becomes a way of being.

Life Now: Integration and Renewal

There was a time when I couldn't imagine feeling peace again. A time when joy felt like something that belonged to other people, like a language I didn't speak. When I was drowning in anxiety, spiraling through panic attacks, and waking up with a knot in my chest every single day, the idea of living with ease felt like a fantasy—something reserved for people who didn't carry the kind of wounds I carried.

And yet, here I am. Writing these words in a body that feels ten years younger than it did five years ago. Waking up without the weight of dread pressing on my lungs. Moving through days with a quiet undercurrent of gratitude that has nothing to do with circumstances and everything to do with the state. Losing twenty pounds without obsessing over scales or starving myself, not because I was chasing aesthetics, but because peace replaced the stress that had been aging me from the inside out. My skin changed. My eyes softened. Even the lines on my face seemed to blur as if life had traced a new map across it—one drawn not in fear, but in flow.

People ask me what I did. Was it a diet? A program? Some secret biohack? And I smile, because the truth is both simpler and harder than anything they expect: I came home. I stopped waging war against my own body. I stopped punishing it with stress hormones by living in perpetual fight-or-flight. I stopped feeding it with processed chaos—whether in the form of toxic food, toxic thoughts, or toxic relationships. And instead, I began to listen. I listened to hunger and fullness, to fatigue and energy, to the subtle whispers that had always been there but drowned beneath the noise of striving.

That listening led me to choices that didn't feel like discipline—they felt like devotion. I ate whole foods because they made me feel alive, not because a diet told me to. I moved my body in ways that brought joy, not in penance for what I ate. I slept—not because I feared illness, but because rest felt sacred, a daily baptism for my nervous system. Slowly, without force, my body recalibrated. Weight melted away like snow in sunlight. Energy returned like a tide I thought had gone out for good. And with it came something even more profound: the sense that my body was no longer my enemy, no longer a problem to fix, but a partner in the dance of being alive.

But the transformation wasn't just physical. It was mental, emotional, and spiritual. The mind that once felt like a hostile landscape—cluttered with worry, riddled with fear—became a garden I could tend with care. The panic that used to hijack my breath gave way to a calm that didn't need to be manufactured because it flowed from a deeper source. Silence stopped feeling like a void and started feeling like a sanctuary. Even the simplest moments—sipping tea, feeling sunlight on my skin, hearing laughter in another room—became enough. More than enough.

And here's the truth I need you to hear: if someone had told me, on that night in the ER when my heart was racing like a trapped bird and my thoughts were screaming that life wasn't worth living, that one day I would wake up joyful, strong, and at peace, I wouldn't have believed them. Not for a second. That night, all I saw was darkness. The sterile lights above me, the sharp smell of antiseptic, the cold certainty that I was broken beyond repair. I didn't want to die, not exactly—but I didn't know how to keep living in the storm I was in. Every breath felt like a negotiation. Every thought felt like an assault. And the weight of it all made oblivion seem like mercy.

But I am here. And if you are reading this, so are you. That matters. The truth is, the night you think will end can become the night that births you. The season that feels like death can become the soil where life takes root. I didn't know that then. I couldn't. But looking back now, I see it clearly: that night wasn't the end. It was the breaking point that opened the door to becoming.

Does this mean life stopped testing me? No. The tests didn't disappear—but I did. Or rather, the version of me that needed control, that clung to certainty, that measured worth in accomplishments—that version dissolved. What remained was presence. And presence changes everything. Because when you stop resisting what is, life stops feeling like a fight. Even in chaos, there is a center. Even in loss, there is a thread of peace that doesn't break.

And here's what I know now: happiness is not a peak you climb. It's not the summit waiting at the end of some grueling ascent. Happiness is a frequency, and like any frequency, you have to tune to it. You don't tune by force. You tune by alignment—by clearing the static of unprocessed emotion, by releasing the interference of rigid beliefs, by softening into the awareness that has been here all along. When you do, happiness stops being conditional. It becomes ambient, woven into the fabric of your days, humming softly beneath every breath.

This is what integration looks like. Not perfection. Not a life without challenge. But a life where the challenges no longer own you because you know who you are beyond them. A life where peace is not an escape from reality but the lens through which you experience it. A life where the external is no longer your compass because the internal has become your home.

And here's the paradox that still makes me smile: all the things I once thought I needed—success, validation, security—they began to flow to me not when I chased them, but when I stopped, when I stopped grasping, when I stopped gripping life by the throat and started letting it breathe through me. Because life responds to frequency, and desperation broadcasts a lack. But presence? Presence hums abundance. And the universe knows that song.

So this is where I live now—not in some static state of bliss, but in a dynamic dance with life. Some days are messy. Some moments hurt. But even in the mess, there is music. Even in the pain, there is presence. And that presence is everything. It's the difference between drowning and floating, between exile and home.

If you're reading this and wondering if it's possible for you, hear me: it is. Not because I'm special, but because what I found isn't exclusive—it's your birthright. The home I came back to is the same home you carry within you now, beneath the noise, beneath the narratives, waiting like a steady flame for you to remember. And when you do—when you taste even a flicker of that truth—everything changes. Not because life suddenly becomes perfect, but because you do.

And this is where the journey circles back to its beginning—not as a loop, but as a spiral, deeper and wider than before. Because coming home isn't the end, it's the beginning of everything that matters. And it starts, as it always has, in the simplest place imaginable: here. Now. In the breath you're taking as you read these words.

The Final Transmission

You've made it here—and that means something. Not just that you read the words, but that you felt them. That you stayed with the discomfort. That you walked through your own fire and didn't flinch. That matters.

But before you go—before you return to the noise and movement of the world—I want to leave you with this:

This book was never just meant to comfort you. It was meant to calibrate you.

Everything you've read has been a mirror—a transmission of energy, vibration, and frequency. Not just concepts, but codes. Reminders. Activations. Because transformation doesn't begin when your life gets easier. It begins when your perception shifts. When you stop giving power to the lies you inherited and start reclaiming your energy from every belief, emotion, and identity that was never yours to begin with.

That's what transmutation is. It's not pretty. It's not clean. It's the process of burning through illusion. Of feeling everything you tried to avoid. Of letting your nervous system speak the truth your mind has been suppressing.

And then—when the fire has stripped away the false—that's when transcendence begins. Not as an escape from the body, but as a rising within it. A realization:

You are not your thoughts. You are not your trauma. You are not your story.

You are the field of awareness, holding it all. And from that field, you can shape reality—not through force, but through coherence.

Because this is the truth no one teaches you:

Your transformation is not about becoming something more.

It's about becoming something clearer.

Something truer.

Something so aligned in frequency that the old timelines simply can't hold you anymore.

This is consciousness in action.

Not just awareness, but applied awareness.

Not just healing, but energetic responsibility.

Not just coming home—but building a new one from the inside out.

So if this book has done its job, then let it end not as a conclusion, but as a beginning.

From this moment forward, don't just remember who you are.

Embody it.

Live it in your breath.

Speak it in your tone.

Move it through your relationships, your purpose, your presence.

Because every time you shift your energy, you shift your reality.

Every time you choose stillness over reactivity, you transmute chaos.

Every time you witness instead of identify, you transcend conditioning.

And every time you come back to presence, you calibrate to truth.

This is a transformation.

Not an event. Not a milestone.

A practice. A frequency. A choice.

Again and again, until it becomes who you are.

And who you are…

has always been powerful enough to change everything.

If you choose to read this book again, do it with intention. Not while driving and listening to the audio book. Not while multitasking. Not when the ego's still running the show and whispering that your worth comes from what you accomplish next. That's the system we're breaking. Sit down. Be still. Hold the book in your hands like something sacred. Feel the weight of it. Let the texture of the page pull you out of survival mode and into presence. Let it disrupt your habits. Let it reset your nervous system. Let it teach your body what stillness actually feels like—because that's where your real transformation begins. By consciously choosing each task and feeling the weight of each decision.

This isn't just a book—it's a mirror.

And some mirrors only speak when you're quiet enough to hear them.

So if you are a leader, let this remind you: real leadership begins with self-mastery.

If you are a parent, know that your vibration becomes your child's emotional climate.

If you are navigating darkness—mental, emotional, spiritual—know that the power to shift it is already within you.

This path is not reserved for the few. It's for anyone brave enough to face their reflection.

So don't just close this book.

Close the gap between who you've been and who you are here to become.

No more hiding behind potential.

No more waiting for the perfect time.

You've got the truth now. You've got the mirror. You've got the map.

Now get up—

and become undeniable and sprout the best version of yourself.

AFTER

September, 2025

California, 2024

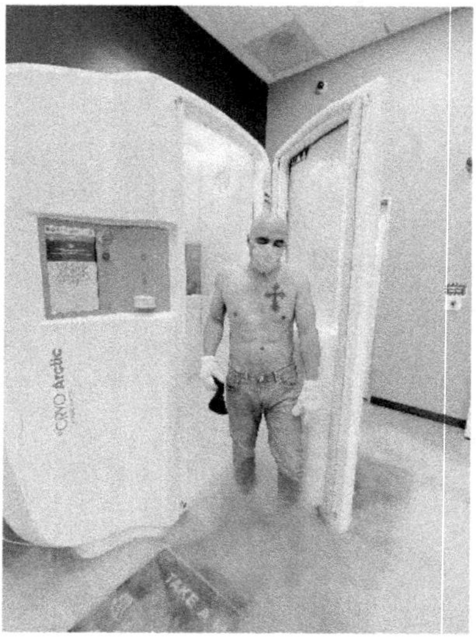

Cryotherapy, 2023

9 Years Old

"Join the Journey"

You've reached the end of the book—

but not the end of the journey.

If you're ready to learn how I freed myself from the constant noise of the mind, how I healed the emotional body, and how you can do the same—

I welcome you to join me.

My private community is a space for conscious growth, honest conversation, and deep transformation.

Together, we learn what it means to live awake.

Join us at www.WithinTheParadox.com

www.ingramcontent.com/pod-product-compliance
Lightning Source LLC
LaVergne TN
LVHW011511200926
848484LV00001B/9
9798295407024